CAMBRIDGE

U0112686

IELTS

剑桥雅思官方真题集

8

WITH ANSWERS

AUTHENTIC PRACTICE TESTS

Produced by Cambridge University Press & Assessment

剑桥大学出版社与考试委员会　编著

QUNYAN PRESS

· 北 京 ·

图书在版编目(CIP)数据

剑桥雅思官方真题集. 8 / 英国剑桥大学出版社与考试委员会编著. -- 北京：群言出版社, 2023.8
书名原文: Cambridge IELTS 8
ISBN 978-7-5193-0855-1

Ⅰ. ①剑… Ⅱ. ①英… Ⅲ. ①IELTS - 习题集 Ⅳ. ①H310.41-44

中国国家版本馆CIP数据核字(2023)第117983号

版权登记：图字01—2023—3080号

责任编辑：孙平平
封面设计：李　倩

出版发行：群言出版社
地　　址：北京市东城区东厂胡同北巷1号（100006）
网　　址：www.qypublish.com（官网书城）
电子信箱：dywh@xdf.cn　qunyancbs@126.com
联系电话：010-62418641　65267783　65263836
法律顾问：北京法政安邦律师事务所
经　　销：全国新华书店

印　　刷：北京华联印刷有限公司
版　　次：2023年8月第1版
印　　次：2023年8月第1次印刷
开　　本：787mm×1092mm　1/16
印　　张：11
字　　数：205千字
书　　号：ISBN 978-7-5193-0855-1
定　　价：128.00元

Contents

Introduction

The International English Language Testing System (IELTS) is widely recognised as a reliable means of assessing the language ability of candidates who need to study or work where English is the language of communication. These Practice Tests are designed to give future IELTS candidates an idea of whether their English is at the required level.

IELTS is owned by three partners, Cambridge University Press & Assessment, part of the University of Cambridge, the British Council and IDP Education Pty Limited (through its subsidiary company, IELTS Australia Pty Limited). Further information on IELTS can be found on the IELTS website www.ielts.org.

WHAT IS THE TEST FORMAT?

IELTS consists of four components. All candidates take the same Listening and Speaking tests. There is a choice of Reading and Writing tests according to whether a candidate is taking the Academic or General Training module.

Academic	General Training
For candidates wishing to study at undergraduate or postgraduate levels, and for those seeking professional registration.	For candidates wishing to migrate to an English-speaking country (Australia, Canada, New Zealand, UK), and for those wishing to train or study at below degree level.

The test components are taken in the following order:

Listening 4 parts, 40 items approximately 30 minutes		
Academic Reading 3 sections, 40 items 60 minutes	or	**General Training Reading** 3 sections, 40 items 60 minutes
Academic Writing 2 tasks 60 minutes	or	**General Training Writing** 2 tasks 60 minutes
Speaking 11 to 14 minutes		
Total Test Time 2 hours 44 minutes		

Listening

This test consists of four parts, each with ten questions. The first two parts are concerned with social needs. The first part is a conversation between two speakers and the second part is a monologue. The final two parts are concerned with situations related to educational or training contexts. The third part is a conversation between up to four people and the fourth part is a monologue.

A variety of question types is used, including: multiple choice, matching, plan/map/diagram labelling, form completion, note completion, table completion, flow-chart completion, summary completion, sentence completion, short-answer questions.

Candidates hear the recording once only and answer the questions as they listen. Ten minutes are allowed at the end for candidates to transfer their answers to the answer sheet.

Academic Reading

This test consists of three sections with 40 questions. There are three texts, which are taken from journals, books, magazines and newspapers. The texts are on topics of general interest. At least one text contains detailed logical argument.

A variety of question types is used, including: multiple choice, identifying information (True/False/Not Given), identifying the writer's views/claims (Yes/No/Not Given), matching information, matching headings, matching features, matching sentence endings, sentence completion, summary completion, note completion, table completion, flow-chart completion, diagram label completion, short-answer questions.

General Training Reading

This test consists of three sections with 40 questions. The texts are taken from notices, advertisements, leaflets, newspapers, instruction manuals, books and magazines. The first section contains texts relevant to basic linguistic survival in English, with tasks mainly concerned with providing factual information. The second section focuses on the work context and involves texts of more complex language. The third section involves reading more extended texts, with a more complex structure, but with the emphasis on descriptive and instructive rather than argumentative texts.

A variety of question types is used, including: multiple choice, identifying information (True/False/Not Given), identifying the writer's views/claims (Yes/No/Not Given), matching information, matching headings, matching features, matching sentence endings, sentence completion, summary completion, note completion, table completion, flow-chart completion, diagram label completion, short-answer questions.

Academic Writing

This test consists of two tasks. It is suggested that candidates spend about 20 minutes on Task 1, which requires them to write at least 150 words, and 40 minutes on Task 2, which requires them to write at least 250 words. Task 2 contributes twice as much as Task 1 to the Writing score.

Task 1 requires candidates to look at a diagram or some data (graph, table or chart) and to present the information in their own words. They are assessed on their ability to organise, present and possibly compare data, describe the stages of a process, describe an object or event, or explain how something works.

In Task 2 candidates are presented with a point of view, argument or problem. They are assessed on their ability to present a solution to the problem, present and justify an opinion, compare and contrast evidence and opinions, evaluate and challenge ideas, evidence or arguments.

Candidates are also assessed on their ability to write in an appropriate style.

General Training Writing

This test consists of two tasks. It is suggested that candidates spend about 20 minutes on Task 1, which requires them to write at least 150 words, and 40 minutes on Task 2, which requires them to write at least 250 words. Task 2 contributes twice as much as Task 1 to the Writing score.

In Task 1 candidates are asked to respond to a given situation with a letter requesting information or explaining the situation. They are assessed on their ability to engage in personal correspondence, elicit and provide general factual information, express needs, wants, likes and dislikes, express opinions, complaints, etc.

In Task 2 candidates are presented with a point of view, argument or problem. They are assessed on their ability to provide general factual information, outline a problem and present a solution, present and justify an opinion, evaluate and challenge ideas, evidence or arguments.

Candidates are also assessed on their ability to write in an appropriate style.

More information on assessing both the Academic and General Training Writing tests, including Writing Assessment Criteria (public version), is available on the IELTS website.

Speaking

This test takes between 11 and 14 minutes and is conducted by a trained examiner. There are three parts:

Part 1

The candidate and the examiner introduce themselves. Candidates then answer general questions about themselves, their home/family, their job/studies, their interests and a wide range of similar familiar topic areas. This part lasts between four and five minutes.

Part 2

The candidate is given a task card with prompts and is asked to talk on a particular topic. The candidate has one minute to prepare and they can make some notes if they wish, before speaking for between one and two minutes. The examiner then asks one or two questions on the same topic.

Part 3

The examiner and the candidate engage in a discussion of more abstract issues which are thematically linked to the topic in Part 2. The discussion lasts between four and five minutes.

The Speaking test assesses whether candidates can communicate effectively in English. The assessment takes into account Fluency and Coherence, Lexical Resource, Grammatical Range and Accuracy, and Pronunciation. More information on assessing the Speaking test, including Speaking Assessment Criteria (public version), is available on the IELTS website.

HOW IS IELTS SCORED?

IELTS results are reported on a nine-band scale. In addition to the score for overall language ability, IELTS provides a score in the form of a profile for each of the four skills (Listening, Reading, Writing and Speaking). These scores are also reported on a nine-band scale. All scores are recorded on the Test Report Form along with details of the candidate's nationality, first language and date of birth. Each Overall Band Score corresponds to a descriptive statement which gives a summary of the English language ability of a candidate classified at that level. The nine bands and their descriptive statements are as follows:

9 Expert User – *Has fully operational command of the language: appropriate, accurate and fluent with complete understanding.*

8 Very Good User – *Has fully operational command of the language with only occasional unsystematic inaccuracies and inappropriacies. Misunderstandings may occur in unfamiliar situations. Handles complex detailed argumentation well.*

7 Good User – *Has operational command of the language, though with occasional inaccuracies, inappropriacies and misunderstandings in some situations. Generally handles complex language well and understands detailed reasoning.*

6 Competent User – *Has generally effective command of the language despite some inaccuracies, inappropriacies and misunderstandings. Can use and understand fairly complex language, particularly in familiar situations.*

5 Modest User – *Has partial command of the language, coping with overall meaning in most situations, though is likely to make many mistakes. Should be able to handle basic communication in own field.*

4 Limited User – *Basic competence is limited to familiar situations. Has frequent problems in understanding and expression. Is not able to use complex language.*

3 Extremely Limited User – *Conveys and understands only general meaning in very familiar situations. Frequent breakdowns in communication occur.*

2 Intermittent User – *No real communication is possible except for the most basic information using isolated words or short formulae in familiar situations and to meet immediate needs. Has great difficulty understanding spoken and written English.*

1 Non User – *Essentially has no ability to use the language beyond possibly a few isolated words.*

0 Did not attempt the test – *No assessable information provided.*

Most universities and colleges in the United Kingdom, Australia, New Zealand, Canada and the USA accept an IELTS Overall Band Score of 6.0 – 7.0 for entry to academic programmes.

MARKING THE PRACTICE TESTS

Listening and Reading

The Answer keys are on pages 152–161.
Each question in the Listening and Reading tests is worth one mark.

Questions which require letter / Roman numeral answers

- For questions where the answers are letters or Roman numerals, you should write *only* the number of answers required. For example, if the answer is a single letter or numeral you should write only one answer. If you have written more letters or numerals than are required, the answer must be marked wrong.

Questions which require answers in the form of words or numbers

- Answers may be written in upper or lower case.
- Words in brackets are *optional* – they are correct, but not necessary.
- Alternative answers are separated by a slash (/).
- If you are asked to write an answer using a certain number of words and/or (a) number(s), you will be penalised if you exceed this. For example, if a question specifies an answer using NO MORE THAN THREE WORDS and the correct answer is 'black leather coat', the answer 'coat of black leather' is *incorrect*.
- In questions where you are expected to complete a gap, you should only transfer the necessary missing word(s) onto the answer sheet. For example, to complete 'in the …', and the correct answer is 'morning', the answer 'in the morning' would be *incorrect*.
- All answers require correct spelling (including words in brackets).
- Both US and UK spelling are acceptable and are included in the Answer Key.
- All standard alternatives for numbers, dates and currencies are acceptable.
- All standard abbreviations are acceptable.
- You will find additional notes about individual answers in the Answer Key.

Writing

The model and sample answers are on pages 162–173. It is not possible for you to give yourself a mark for the Writing tasks. For Task 2 in Tests 1 and 3, and Task 1 in Tests 2 and 4, and for Task 1 in General Training Test A and Task 2 in General Training Test B, we have provided model answers (written by an examiner). It is important to note that these show just one way of completing the task, out of many possible approaches. For Task 1 in Tests 1 and 3, and Task 2 in Tests 2 and 4, and for Task 2 in General Training Test A and Task 1 in General Training Test B, we have provided sample answers (written by candidates), showing their score and the examiner's comments. These model answers and sample answers will give you an insight into what is required for the Writing test.

HOW SHOULD YOU INTERPRET YOUR SCORES?

At the end of the each Listening and Reading Answer key you will find a chart which will help you assess whether, on the basis of your Practice Test results, you are ready to take the IELTS test.

In interpreting your score, there are a number of points you should bear in mind. Your performance in the real IELTS test will be reported in two ways: there will be a Band Score from 1 to 9 for each of the components and an Overall Band Score from 1 to 9, which is the average of your scores in the four components. However, institutions considering your application are advised to look at both the Overall Band Score and the Bands for each component in order to determine whether you have the language skills needed for a particular course of study. For example, if your course has a lot of reading and writing, but no lectures, listening skills might be less important and a score of 5 in Listening might be acceptable if the Overall Band Score was 7. However, for a course which has lots of lectures and spoken instructions, a score of 5 in Listening might be unacceptable even though the Overall Band Score was 7.

Once you have marked your tests you should have some idea of whether your listening and reading skills are good enough for you to try the IELTS test. If you did well enough in one component but not in others, you will have to decide for yourself whether you are ready to take the test.

The Practice Tests have been checked to ensure that they are of approximately the same level of difficulty as the real IELTS test. However, we cannot guarantee that your score in the Practice Tests will be reflected in the real IELTS test. The Practice Tests can only give you an idea of your possible future performance and it is ultimately up to you to make decisions based on your score.

Different institutions accept different IELTS scores for different types of courses. We have based our recommendations on the average scores which the majority of institutions accept. The institution to which you are applying may, of course, require a higher or lower score than most other institutions.

Further information

For more information about IELTS or any other Cambridge English Qualification, write to:

Cambridge University Press & Assessment
Shaftesbury Road
Cambridge
CB2 8EA
United Kingdom

Telephone: +44 1223 553311
www.cambridgeenglish.org
http://www.ielts.org

Test 1

PART 1   *Questions 1–10*

Questions 1 and 2

Choose the correct letter, A, B or C.

1   In the lobby of the library George saw

    A   a group playing music.
    B   a display of instruments.
    C   a video about the festival.

2   George wants to sit at the back so they can

    A   see well.
    B   hear clearly.
    C   pay less.

Questions 3–10

Complete the form below.

Write **NO MORE THAN TWO WORDS AND/OR A NUMBER** *for each answer.*

SUMMER MUSIC FESTIVAL BOOKING FORM		

NAME: George O'Neill

ADDRESS: **3** ...., Westsea

POSTCODE: **4** ....

TELEPHONE: **5** ....

Date	Event	Price per ticket	No. of tickets
5 June	Instrumental group – *Guitarrini*	£7.50	2
17 June	Singer (price includes **6** .... in the garden)	£6	2
22 June	**7** .... (Anna Ventura)	£7.00	1
23 June	Spanish Dance & Guitar Concert	**8** £	**9** ....

NB Children / Students / Senior Citizens have **10** .... discount on all tickets.

PART 2   *Questions 11–20*

Questions 11–15

Complete the sentences below.

Write **NO MORE THAN TWO WORDS AND/OR A NUMBER** *for each answer.*

The Dinosaur Museum

11 The museum closes at .... p.m. on Mondays.

12 The museum is not open on ....

13 School groups are met by tour guides in the ....

14 The whole visit takes 90 minutes, including .... minutes for the guided tour.

15 There are .... behind the museum where students can have lunch.

Questions 16–18

*Choose **THREE** letters, **A–G**.*

Which **THREE** things can students have with them in the museum?

    A   food
    B   water
    C   cameras
    D   books
    E   bags
    F   pens
    G   worksheets

Questions 19 and 20

*Choose **TWO** letters, **A–E**.*

Which **TWO** activities can students do after the tour at present?

  A build model dinosaurs
  B watch films
  C draw dinosaurs
  D find dinosaur eggs
  E play computer games

PART 3   *Questions 21–30*

Questions 21–24

*Choose the correct letter, **A**, **B** or **C**.*

Field Trip Proposal

21   The tutor thinks that Sandra's proposal

    A   should be re-ordered in some parts.
    B   needs a contents page.
    C   ought to include more information.

22   The proposal would be easier to follow if Sandra

    A   inserted subheadings.
    B   used more paragraphs.
    C   shortened her sentences.

23   What was the problem with the formatting on Sandra's proposal?

    A   Separate points were not clearly identified.
    B   The headings were not always clear.
    C   Page numbering was not used in an appropriate way.

24   Sandra became interested in visiting the Navajo National Park through

    A   articles she read.
    B   movies she saw as a child.
    C   photographs she found on the internet.

Questions 25–27

*Choose **THREE** letters, **A–G**.*

Which **THREE** topics does Sandra agree to include in the proposal?

    A   climate change
    B   field trip activities
    C   geographical features
    D   impact of tourism
    E   myths and legends
    F   plant and animal life
    G   social history

Questions 28–30

Complete the sentences below.

*Write **ONE WORD AND/OR A NUMBER** for each answer.*

28   The tribal park covers .... hectares.

29   Sandra suggests that they share the .... for transport.

30   She says they could also explore the local ....

PART 4   *Questions 31–40*

Complete the notes below.

*Write **ONE WORD ONLY** for each answer.*

Geography

Studying geography helps us to understand:

- the effects of different processes on the **31** .... of the Earth
- the dynamic between **32** .... and population

Two main branches of study:

- physical features
- human lifestyles and their **33** ....

Specific study areas: biophysical, topographic, political, social, economic, historical and **34** .... geography, and also cartography

Key point: geography helps us to understand our surroundings and the associated **35** ....

What do geographers do?

- find data – e.g. conduct censuses, collect information in the form of **36** .... using computer and satellite technology
- analyse data – identify **37** ...., e.g. cause and effect

- publish findings in form of:

  a) maps

    - easy to carry
    - can show physical features of large and small areas
    - BUT a two-dimensional map will always have some **38** ....

  b) aerial photos

    - can show vegetation problems, **39** .... density, ocean floor etc.

  c) Landsat pictures sent to receiving stations

    - used for monitoring **40** .... conditions etc.

READING

READING PASSAGE 1

*You should spend about 20 minutes on **Questions 1–13**, which are based on Reading Passage 1 below.*

A Chronicle of Timekeeping

Our conception of time depends on the way we measure it

A   According to archaeological evidence, at least 5,000 years ago, and long before the advent of the Roman Empire, the Babylonians began to measure time, introducing calendars to co-ordinate communal activities, to plan the shipment of goods and, in particular, to regulate planting and harvesting. They based their calendars on three natural cycles: the solar day, marked by the successive periods of light and darkness as the earth rotates on its axis; the lunar month, following the phases of the moon as it orbits the earth; and the solar year, defined by the changing seasons that accompany our planet's revolution around the sun.

B   Before the invention of artificial light, the moon had greater social impact. And, for those living near the equator in particular, its waxing and waning was more conspicuous than the passing of the seasons. Hence, the calendars that were developed at the lower latitudes were influenced more by the lunar cycle than by the solar year. In more northern climes, however, where seasonal agriculture was practised, the solar year became more crucial. As the Roman Empire expanded northward, it organised its activity chart for the most part around the solar year.

C   Centuries before the Roman Empire, the Egyptians had formulated a municipal calendar having 12 months of 30 days, with five days added to approximate the solar year. Each period of ten days was marked by the appearance of special groups of stars called decans. At the rise of the star Sirius just before sunrise, which occurred around the all-important annual flooding of the Nile, 12 decans could be seen spanning the heavens. The cosmic significance the Egyptians placed in the 12 decans led them to develop a system in which each interval of darkness (and later, each interval of daylight) was divided into a dozen equal parts. These periods became known as temporal hours because their duration varied according to the changing length of days and nights with the passing of the seasons. Summer hours were long, winter ones short; only at the spring and autumn equinoxes were the hours of daylight and darkness equal. Temporal hours, which were first adopted by the Greeks and then the Romans, who disseminated them through Europe, remained in use for more than 2,500 years.

D In order to track temporal hours during the day, inventors created sundials, which indicate time by the length or direction of the sun's shadow. The sundial's counterpart, the water clock, was designed to measure temporal hours at night. One of the first water clocks was a basin with a small hole near the bottom through which the water dripped out. The falling water level denoted the passing hour as it dipped below hour lines inscribed on the inner surface. Although these devices performed satisfactorily around the Mediterranean, they could not always be depended on in the cloudy and often freezing weather of northern Europe.

E The advent of the mechanical clock meant that although it could be adjusted to maintain temporal hours, it was naturally suited to keeping equal ones. With these, however, arose the question of when to begin counting, and so, in the early 14th century, a number of systems evolved. The schemes that divided the day into 24 equal parts varied according to the start of the count: Italian hours began at sunset, Babylonian hours at sunrise, astronomical hours at midday and 'great clock' hours, used for some large public clocks in Germany, at midnight. Eventually these were superseded by 'small clock', or French, hours, which split the day into two 12-hour periods commencing at midnight.

F The earliest recorded weight-driven mechanical clock was built in 1283 in Bedfordshire in England. The revolutionary aspect of this new timekeeper was neither the descending weight that provided its motive force nor the gear wheels (which had been around for at least 1,300 years) that transferred the power; it was the part called the escapement. In the early 1400s came the invention of the coiled spring or fusee which maintained constant force to the gear wheels of the timekeeper despite the changing tension of its mainspring. By the 16th century, a pendulum clock had been devised, but the pendulum swung in a large arc and thus was not very efficient.

G To address this, a variation on the original escapement was invented in 1670, in England. It was called the anchor escapement, which was a lever-based device shaped like a ship's anchor. The motion of a pendulum rocks this device so that it catches and then releases each tooth of the escape wheel, in turn allowing it to turn a precise amount. Unlike the original form used in early pendulum clocks, the anchor escapement permitted the pendulum to travel in a very small arc. Moreover, this invention allowed the use of a long pendulum which could beat once a second and thus led to the development of a new floor-standing case design, which became known as the grandfather clock.

H Today, highly accurate timekeeping instruments set the beat for most electronic devices. Nearly all computers contain a quartz-crystal clock to regulate their operation. Moreover, not only do time signals beamed down from Global Positioning System satellites calibrate the functions of precision navigation equipment, they do so as well for mobile phones, instant stock-trading systems and nationwide power-distribution grids. So integral have these time-based technologies become to day-to-day existence that our dependency on them is recognised only when they fail to work.

Questions 1–4

Reading Passage 1 has eight paragraphs, **A–H**.

Which paragraph contains the following information?

*Write the correct letter, **A–H**, in boxes 1–4 on your answer sheet.*

1   a description of an early timekeeping invention affected by cold temperatures

2   an explanation of the importance of geography in the development of the calendar in farming communities

3   a description of the origins of the pendulum clock

4   details of the simultaneous efforts of different societies to calculate time using uniform hours

Questions 5–8

Look at the following events (Questions 5–8) and the list of nationalities below.

*Match each event with the correct nationality, **A–F**.*

*Write the correct letter, **A–F**, in boxes 5–8 on your answer sheet.*

5   They devised a civil calendar in which the months were equal in length.

6   They divided the day into two equal halves.

7   They developed a new cabinet shape for a type of timekeeper.

8   They created a calendar to organise public events and work schedules.

List of Nationalities
A   Babylonians
B   Egyptians
C   Greeks
D   English
E   Germans
F   French

Questions 9–13

Label the diagram below.

*Choose **NO MORE THAN TWO WORDS** from the passage for each answer.*

Write your answers in boxes 9–13 on your answer sheet.

How the 1670 lever-based device worked

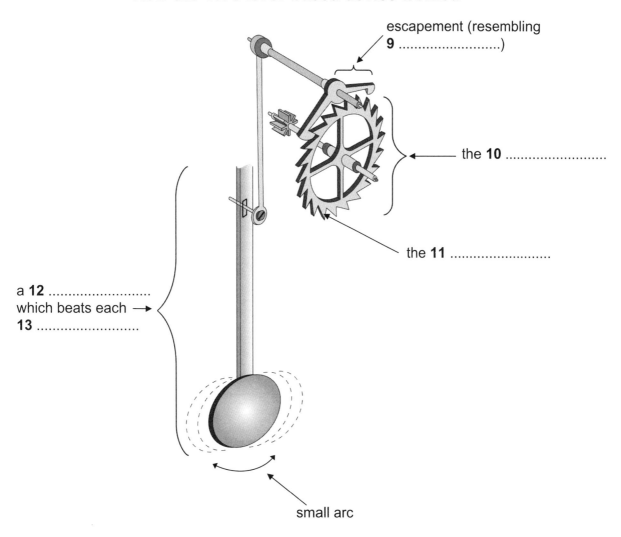

escapement (resembling
9 ....)

the **10** ....

the **11** ....

a **12** ....
which beats each →
13 ....

small arc

READING PASSAGE 2

*You should spend about 20 minutes on **Questions 14–26**, which are based on Reading Passage 2 on the following pages.*

Questions 14–19

Reading Passage 2 has seven paragraphs, **A–G**.

*Choose the correct heading for paragraphs **A** and **C–G** from the list below.*

*Write the correct number, **i–x**, in boxes 14–19 on your answer sheet.*

List of Headings
i   Disobeying FAA regulations
ii   Aviation disaster prompts action
iii   Two coincidental developments
iv   Setting altitude zones
v   An oversimplified view
vi   Controlling pilots' licences
vii   Defining airspace categories
viii   Setting rules to weather conditions
ix   Taking off safely
x   First steps towards ATC

14   Paragraph **A**

Example	Answer
Paragraph B	**x**

15   Paragraph **C**

16   Paragraph **D**

17   Paragraph **E**

18   Paragraph **F**

19   Paragraph **G**

AIR TRAFFIC CONTROL IN THE USA

A   An accident that occurred in the skies over the Grand Canyon in 1956 resulted in the establishment of the Federal Aviation Administration (FAA) to regulate and oversee the operation of aircraft in the skies over the United States, which were becoming quite congested. The resulting structure of air traffic control has greatly increased the safety of flight in the United States, and similar air traffic control procedures are also in place over much of the rest of the world.

B   Rudimentary air traffic control (ATC) existed well before the Grand Canyon disaster. As early as the 1920s, the earliest air traffic controllers manually guided aircraft in the vicinity of the airports, using lights and flags, while beacons and flashing lights were placed along cross-country routes to establish the earliest airways. However, this purely visual system was useless in bad weather, and, by the 1930s, radio communication was coming into use for ATC. The first region to have something approximating today's ATC was New York City, with other major metropolitan areas following soon after.

C   In the 1940s, ATC centres could and did take advantage of the newly developed radar and improved radio communication brought about by the Second World War, but the system remained rudimentary. It was only after the creation of the FAA that full-scale regulation of America's airspace took place, and this was fortuitous, for the advent of the jet engine suddenly resulted in a large number of very fast planes, reducing pilots' margin of error and practically demanding some set of rules to keep everyone well separated and operating safely in the air.

D   Many people think that ATC consists of a row of controllers sitting in front of their radar screens at the nation's airports, telling arriving and departing traffic what to do. This is a very incomplete part of the picture. The FAA realised that the airspace over the United States would at any time have many different kinds of planes, flying for many different purposes, in a variety of weather conditions, and the same kind of structure was needed to accommodate all of them.

E   To meet this challenge, the following elements were put into effect. First, ATC extends over virtually the entire United States. In general, from 365m above the ground and higher, the entire country is blanketed by controlled airspace. In certain areas, mainly near airports, controlled airspace extends down to 215m above the ground, and, in the immediate vicinity of an airport, all the way down to the surface. Controlled airspace is that airspace in which FAA regulations apply. Elsewhere, in uncontrolled airspace, pilots are bound by fewer regulations. In this way, the recreational pilot who simply wishes to go flying for a while without all the

23

restrictions imposed by the FAA has only to stay in uncontrolled airspace, below 365m, while the pilot who does want the protection afforded by ATC can easily enter the controlled airspace.

F The FAA then recognised two types of operating environments. In good meteorological conditions, flying would be permitted under Visual Flight Rules (VFR), which suggests a strong reliance on visual cues to maintain an acceptable level of safety. Poor visibility necessitated a set of Instrumental Flight Rules (IFR), under which the pilot relied on altitude and navigational information provided by the plane's instrument panel to fly safely. On a clear day, a pilot in controlled airspace can choose a VFR or IFR flight plan, and the FAA regulations were devised in a way which accommodates both VFR and IFR operations in the same airspace. However, a pilot can only choose to fly IFR if they possess an instrument rating which is above and beyond the basic pilot's license that must also be held.

G Controlled airspace is divided into several different types, designated by letters of the alphabet. Uncontrolled airspace is designated Class F, while controlled airspace below 5,490m above sea level and not in the vicinity of an airport is Class E. All airspace above 5,490m is designated Class A. The reason for the division of Class E and Class A airspace stems from the type of planes operating in them. Generally, Class E airspace is where one finds general aviation aircraft (few of which can climb above 5,490m anyway), and commercial turboprop aircraft. Above 5,490m is the realm of the heavy jets, since jet engines operate more efficiently at higher altitudes. The difference between Class E and A airspace is that in Class A, all operations are IFR, and pilots must be instrument-rated, that is, skilled and licensed in aircraft instrumentation. This is because ATC control of the entire space is essential. Three other types of airspace, Classes D, C and B, govern the vicinity of airports. These correspond roughly to small municipal, medium-sized metropolitan and major metropolitan airports respectively, and encompass an increasingly rigorous set of regulations. For example, all a VFR pilot has to do to enter Class C airspace is establish two-way radio contact with ATC. No explicit permission from ATC to enter is needed, although the pilot must continue to obey all regulations governing VFR flight. To enter Class B airspace, such as on approach to a major metropolitan airport, an explicit ATC clearance is required. The private pilot who cruises without permission into this airspace risks losing their license.

Questions 20–26

Do the following statements agree with the information given in Reading Passage 2?

In boxes 20–26 on your answer sheet, write

TRUE   *if the statement agrees with the information*
FALSE   *if the statement contradicts the information*
NOT GIVEN   *if there is no information on this*

20   The FAA was created as a result of the introduction of the jet engine.

21   Air Traffic Control started after the Grand Canyon crash in 1956.

22   Beacons and flashing lights are still used by ATC today.

23   Some improvements were made in radio communication during World War II.

24   Class F airspace is airspace which is below 365m and not near airports.

25   All aircraft in Class E airspace must use IFR.

26   A pilot entering Class C airspace is flying over an average-sized city.

READING PASSAGE 3

*You should spend about 20 minutes on **Questions 27–40**, which are based on Reading Passage 3 below.*

Can human beings communicate by thought alone? For more than a century the issue of telepathy has divided the scientific community, and even today it still sparks bitter controversy among top academics

Since the 1970s, parapsychologists at leading universities and research institutes around the world have risked the derision of sceptical colleagues by putting the various claims for telepathy to the test in dozens of rigorous scientific studies. The results and their implications are dividing even the researchers who uncovered them.

Some researchers say the results constitute compelling evidence that telepathy is genuine. Other parapsychologists believe the field is on the brink of collapse, having tried to produce definitive scientific proof and failed. Sceptics and advocates alike do concur on one issue, however: that the most impressive evidence so far has come from the so-called 'ganzfeld' experiments, a German term that means 'whole field'. Reports of telepathic experiences had by people during meditation led parapsychologists to suspect that telepathy might involve 'signals' passing between people that were so faint that they were usually swamped by normal brain activity. In this case, such signals might be more easily detected by those experiencing meditation-like tranquillity in a relaxing 'whole field' of light, sound and warmth.

The ganzfeld experiment tries to recreate these conditions with participants sitting in soft reclining chairs in a sealed room, listening to relaxing sounds while their eyes are covered with special filters letting in only soft pink light. In early ganzfeld experiments, the telepathy test involved identification of a picture chosen from a random selection of four taken from a large image bank. The idea was that a person acting as a 'sender' would attempt to beam the image over to the 'receiver' relaxing in the sealed room. Once the session was over, this person was asked to identify which of the four images had been used. Random guessing would give a hit-rate of 25 per cent; if telepathy is real, however, the hit-rate would be higher. In 1982, the results from the first ganzfeld studies were analysed by one of its pioneers, the American parapsychologist Charles Honorton. They pointed to typical hit-rates of better than 30 per cent – a small effect, but one which statistical tests suggested could not be put down to chance.

The implication was that the ganzfeld method had revealed real evidence for telepathy. But there was a crucial flaw in this argument – one routinely overlooked in more conventional areas of science. Just because chance had been ruled out as an explanation did not prove telepathy must exist; there were many other ways of getting positive results. These ranged from 'sensory leakage' – where clues about the pictures accidentally reach the receiver – to outright fraud. In response, the researchers issued a review of all the ganzfeld studies done up to 1985 to show that 80 per cent had found statistically significant evidence. However, they also agreed that there were still too many problems in the experiments which could lead to positive results, and they drew up a list demanding new standards for future research.

After this, many researchers switched to autoganzfeld tests – an automated variant of the technique which used computers to perform many of the key tasks such as the random selection of images. By minimising human involvement, the idea was to minimise the risk of flawed results. In 1987, results from hundreds of autoganzfeld tests were studied by Honorton in a 'meta-analysis', a statistical technique for finding the overall results from a set of studies. Though less compelling than before, the outcome was still impressive.

Yet some parapsychologists remain disturbed by the lack of consistency between individual ganzfeld studies. Defenders of telepathy point out that demanding impressive evidence from every study ignores one basic statistical fact: it takes large samples to detect small effects. If, as current results suggest, telepathy produces hit-rates only marginally above the 25 per cent expected by chance, it's unlikely to be detected by a typical ganzfeld study involving around 40 people: the group is just not big enough. Only when many studies are combined in a meta-analysis will the faint signal of telepathy really become apparent. And that is what researchers do seem to be finding.

What they are certainly not finding, however, is any change in attitude of mainstream scientists: most still totally reject the very idea of telepathy. The problem stems at least in part from the lack of any plausible mechanism for telepathy.

Various theories have been put forward, many focusing on esoteric ideas from theoretical physics. They include 'quantum entanglement', in which events affecting one group of atoms instantly affect another group, no matter how far apart they may be. While physicists have demonstrated entanglement with specially prepared atoms, no-one knows if it also exists between atoms making up human minds. Answering such questions would transform parapsychology. This has prompted some researchers to argue that the future lies not in collecting more evidence for telepathy, but in probing possible mechanisms. Some work has begun already, with researchers trying to identify people who are particularly successful in autoganzfeld trials. Early results show that creative and artistic people do much better than average: in one study at the University of Edinburgh, musicians achieved a hit-rate of 56 per cent. Perhaps more tests like these will eventually give the researchers the evidence they are seeking and strengthen the case for the existence of telepathy.

Questions 27–30

*Complete each sentence with the correct ending, **A–G**, below.*

*Write the correct letter, **A–G**, in boxes 27–30 on your answer sheet.*

27   Researchers with differing attitudes towards telepathy agree on

28   Reports of experiences during meditation indicated

29   Attitudes to parapsychology would alter drastically with

30   Recent autoganzfeld trials suggest that success rates will improve with

A	the discovery of a mechanism for telepathy.
B	the need to create a suitable environment for telepathy.
C	their claims of a high success rate.
D	a solution to the problem posed by random guessing.
E	the significance of the ganzfeld experiments.
F	a more careful selection of subjects.
G	a need to keep altering conditions.

Questions 31–40

Complete the table below.

*Choose **NO MORE THAN THREE WORDS** from the passage for each answer.*

Write your answers in boxes 31–40 on your answer sheet.

Telepathy Experiments			
Name/Date	**Description**	**Result**	**Flaw**
Ganzfeld studies 1982	Involved a person acting as a **31** .... , who picked out one **32** .... from a random selection of four, and a **33** .... , who then tried to identify it.	Hit-rates were higher than with random guessing.	Positive results could be produced by factors such as **34** .... or **35** ....
Autoganzfeld studies 1987	**36** .... were used for key tasks to limit the amount of **37** .... in carrying out the tests.	The results were then subjected to a **38**	The **39** .... between different test results was put down to the fact that sample groups were not **40** .... (as with most ganzfeld studies).

WRITING

WRITING TASK 1

You should spend about 20 minutes on this task.

The pie chart below shows the main reasons why agricultural land becomes less productive. The table shows how these causes affected three regions of the world during the 1990s.

Summarise the information by selecting and reporting the main features, and make comparisons where relevant.

Write at least 150 words.

Causes of worldwide land degradation

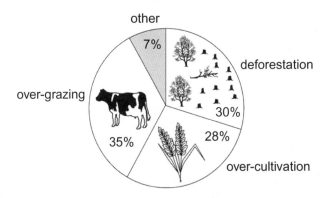

Causes of land degradation by region

Region	% land degraded by...			
	deforestation	over-cultivation	over-grazing	Total land degraded
North America	0.2	3.3	1.5	5%
Europe	9.8	7.7	5.5	23%
Oceania*	1.7	0	11.3	13%

* A large group of islands in the South Pacific including Australia and New Zealand

WRITING TASK 2

You should spend about 40 minutes on this task.

Write about the following topic:

> *Some people think that parents should teach children how to be good members of society. Others, however, believe that school is the place to learn this.*
>
> *Discuss both these views and give your own opinion.*

Give reasons for your answer and include any relevant examples from your own knowledge or experience.

Write at least 250 words.

SPEAKING

PART 1

The examiner asks the candidate about him/herself, his/her home, work or studies and other familiar topics.

EXAMPLE

Neighbours

- How well do you know the people who live next door to you?
- How often do you see them? [Why/Why not?]
- What kinds of problem do people sometimes have with their neighbours?
- How do you think neighbours can help each other?

PART 2

Describe a time when you were asked to give your opinion in a questionnaire or survey
 	
You should say:
    what the questionnaire/survey was about
    why you were asked to give your opinions
    what opinions you gave
and explain how you felt about giving your opinions in this questionnaire/survey.

You will have to talk about the topic for one to two minutes. You have one minute to think about what you are going to say. You can make some notes to help you if you wish.

PART 3

Discussion topics:

Asking questions

Example questions:
What kinds of organisation want to find out about people's opinions?
Do you think that questionnaires or surveys are good ways of finding out people's opinions?
What reasons might people have for not wanting to give their opinions?

Questionnaires in school

Example questions:
Do you think it would be a good idea for schools to ask students their opinions about lessons?
What would the advantages for schools be if they asked students their opinions?
Would there be any disadvantages in asking students' opinions?

Test 2

PART 1   *Questions 1–10*

Questions 1–3

Complete the form below.

*Write **NO MORE THAN THREE WORDS AND/OR A NUMBER** for each answer.*

TOTAL INSURANCE INCIDENT REPORT

Name	Michael Alexander
Address	24 Manly Street, **1** .... , Sydney
Shipping agent	**2** ....
Place of origin	China
Date of arrival	**3** ....
Reference number	601 ACK

Questions 4–10

Complete the table below.

Write **ONE WORD AND/OR A NUMBER** for each answer.

Item	Damage	Cost to repair/ replace
Television	The **4** .... needs to be replaced	not known
The **5** .... cabinet	The **6** .... of the cabinet is damaged	**7** $ ....
Dining room table	A **8** .... is split	$200
Set of china	Six **9** .... were broken	about **10** $ .... in total

PART 2   *Questions 11–20*

Question 11

*Choose the correct letter, **A**, **B** or **C**.*

11   According to the speaker, the main purposes of the park are

    A   education and entertainment.
    B   research and education.
    C   research and entertainment.

Questions 12–14

Label the plan below.

*Write **NO MORE THAN TWO WORDS** for each answer.*

Agricultural Park

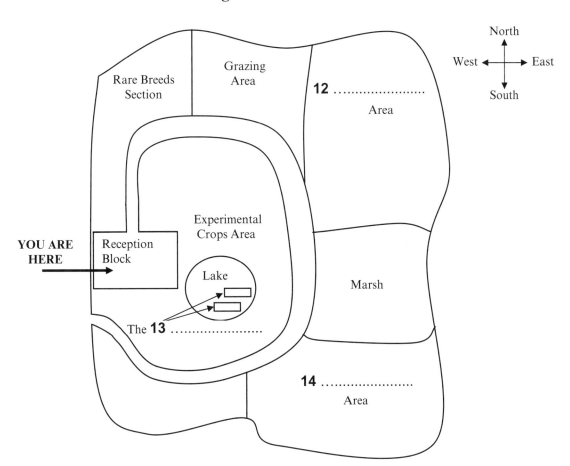

Questions 15–20

*Choose the correct letter, **A**, **B** or **C**.*

15 When are the experimental areas closed to the public?

A all the year round
B almost all the year
C a short time every year

16 How can you move around the park?

A by tram, walking or bicycle
B by solar car or bicycle
C by bicycle, walking or bus

17 The rare breed animals kept in the park include

A hens and horses.
B goats and cows.
C goats and hens.

18 What is the main purpose of having the Rare Breeds Section?

A to save unusual animals
B to keep a variety of breeds
C to educate the public

19 What can you see in the park at the present time?

A the arrival of wild birds
B fruit tree blossom
C a demonstration of fishing

20 The shop contains books about

A animals.
B local traditions.
C the history of the park.

PART 3   *Questions 21–30*

Questions 21–24

Choose the correct letter, A, B or C.

Honey Bees in Australia

21   Where in Australia have Asian honey bees been found in the past?

A   Queensland
B   New South Wales
C   several states

22   A problem with Asian honey bees is that they

A   attack native bees.
B   carry parasites.
C   damage crops.

23   What point is made about Australian bees?

A   Their honey varies in quality.
B   Their size stops them from pollinating some flowers.
C   They are sold to customers abroad.

24   Grant Freeman says that if Asian honey bees got into Australia,

A   the country's economy would be affected.
B   they could be used in the study of allergies.
C   certain areas of agriculture would benefit.

Questions 25–30

Complete the summary below.

*Write **ONE WORD ONLY** for each answer.*

Looking for Asian honey bees

Birds called Rainbow Bee Eaters eat only **25** ….................... , and cough up small bits of skeleton and other products in a pellet.

Researchers go to the locations the bee eaters like to use for **26** ….................... .
They collect the pellets and take them to a **27** ….................... for analysis.
Here **28** ….................... is used to soften them, and the researchers look for the **29** ….................... of Asian bees in the pellets.

The benefit of this research is that the result is more **30** ….................... than searching for live Asian bees.

PART 4   *Questions 31–40*

Questions 31–36

*Choose the correct letter, **A**, **B** or **C**.*

Research on questions about doctors

31 In order to set up her research programme, Shona got

    A advice from personal friends in other countries.
    B help from students in other countries.
    C information from her tutor's contacts in other countries.

32 What types of people were included in the research?

    A young people in their first job
    B men who were working
    C women who were unemployed

33 Shona says that in her questionnaire her aim was

    A to get a wide range of data.
    B to limit people's responses.
    C to guide people through interviews.

34 What do Shona's initial results show about medical services in Britain?

    A Current concerns are misrepresented by the press.
    B Financial issues are critical to the government.
    C Reforms within hospitals have been unsuccessful.

35 Shona needs to do further research in order to

    A present the government with her findings.
    B decide the level of extra funding needed.
    C identify the preferences of the public.

36 Shona has learnt from the research project that

    A it is important to plan projects carefully.
    B people do not like answering questions.
    C colleagues do not always agree.

Questions 37–40

Which statement applies to each of the following people who were interviewed by Shona?

*Choose **FOUR** answers from the box and write the correct letter, **A–F**, next to questions 37–40.*

A	gave false data
B	decided to stop participating
C	refused to tell Shona about their job
D	kept changing their mind about participating
E	became very angry with Shona
F	was worried about confidentiality

People interviewed by Shona

37 a person interviewed in the street   ....

38 an undergraduate at the university   ....

39 a colleague in her department   ....

40 a tutor in a foreign university   ....

READING

READING PASSAGE 1

*You should spend about 20 minutes on **Questions 1–13**, which are based on Reading Passage 1 below.*

Sheet glass manufacture: the float process

Glass, which has been made since the time of the Mesopotamians and Egyptians, is little more than a mixture of sand, soda ash and lime. When heated to about 1500 degrees Celsius (°C) this becomes a molten mass that hardens when slowly cooled. The first successful method for making clear, flat glass involved spinning. This method was very effective as the glass had not touched any surfaces between being soft and becoming hard, so it stayed perfectly unblemished, with a 'fire finish'. However, the process took a long time and was labour intensive.

Nevertheless, demand for flat glass was very high and glassmakers across the world were looking for a method of making it continuously. The first continuous ribbon process involved squeezing molten glass through two hot rollers, similar to an old mangle. This allowed glass of virtually any thickness to be made non-stop, but the rollers would leave both sides of the glass marked, and these would then need to be ground and polished. This part of the process rubbed away around 20 per cent of the glass, and the machines were very expensive.

The float process for making flat glass was invented by Alistair Pilkington. This process allows the manufacture of clear, tinted and coated glass for buildings, and clear and tinted glass for vehicles. Pilkington had been experimenting with improving the melting process, and in 1952 he had the idea of using a bed of molten metal to form the flat glass, eliminating altogether the need for rollers within the float bath. The metal had to melt at a temperature less than the hardening point of glass (about 600°C), but could not boil at a temperature below the temperature of the molten glass (about 1500°C). The best metal for the job was tin.

The rest of the concept relied on gravity, which guaranteed that the surface of the molten metal was perfectly flat and horizontal. Consequently, when pouring molten glass onto the molten tin, the underside of the glass would also be perfectly flat. If the glass were kept hot enough, it would flow over the molten tin until the top surface was also flat, horizontal and perfectly parallel to the bottom surface. Once the glass cooled to 604°C or less it was too hard to mark and could be transported out of the cooling zone by rollers. The glass settled to a thickness of six millimetres because of surface tension interactions between the glass and the tin. By fortunate coincidence, 60 per cent of the flat glass market at that time was for six-millimetre glass.

Pilkington built a pilot plant in 1953 and by 1955 he had convinced his company to build a full-scale plant. However, it took 14 months of non-stop production, costing the company £100,000 a month, before the plant produced any usable glass. Furthermore, once they succeeded in making marketable flat glass, the machine was turned off for a service to prepare it for years of continuous production. When it started up again it took another four months to get the process right again. They finally succeeded in 1959 and there are now float plants all over the world, with each able to produce around 1000 tons of glass every day, non-stop for around 15 years.

Float plants today make glass of near optical quality. Several processes – melting, refining, homogenising – take place simultaneously in the 2000 tonnes of molten glass in the furnace. They occur in separate zones in a complex glass flow driven by high temperatures. It adds up to a continuous melting process, lasting as long as 50 hours, that delivers glass smoothly and continuously to the float bath, and from there to a coating zone and finally a heat treatment zone, where stresses formed during cooling are relieved.

The principle of float glass is unchanged since the 1950s. However, the product has changed dramatically, from a single thickness of 6.8 mm to a range from sub-millimetre to 25 mm, from a ribbon frequently marred by inclusions and bubbles to almost optical perfection. To ensure the highest quality, inspection takes place at every stage. Occasionally, a bubble is not removed during refining, a sand grain refuses to melt, a tremor in the tin puts ripples into the glass ribbon. Automated on-line inspection does two things. Firstly, it reveals process faults upstream that can be corrected. Inspection technology allows more than 100 million measurements a second to be made across the ribbon, locating flaws the unaided eye would be unable to see. Secondly, it enables computers downstream to steer cutters around flaws.

Float glass is sold by the square metre, and at the final stage computers translate customer requirements into patterns of cuts designed to minimise waste.

Questions 1–8

Complete the table and diagram below.

*Choose **NO MORE THAN TWO WORDS** from the passage for each answer.*

Write your answers in boxes 1–8 on your answer sheet.

Early methods of producing flat glass

Method	Advantages	Disadvantages
1	• Glass remained **2**	• Slow • **3** ....
Ribbon	• Could produce glass sheets of varying **4** .... • Non-stop process	• Glass was **5** .... • 20% of glass rubbed away • Machines were expensive

Pilkington's float process

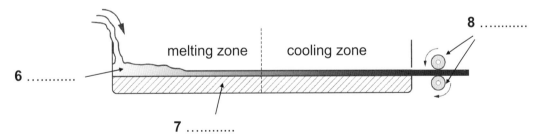

8 ....

melting zone   cooling zone

6 ....

7 ....

Questions 9–13

Do the following statements agree with the information given in Reading Passage 1?

In boxes 9–13 on your answer sheet, write

TRUE	*if the statement agrees with the information*
FALSE	*if the statement contradicts the information*
NOT GIVEN	*if there is no information on this*

9 The metal used in the float process had to have specific properties.

10 Pilkington invested some of his own money in his float plant.

11 Pilkington's first full-scale plant was an instant commercial success.

12 The process invented by Pilkington has now been improved.

13 Computers are better than humans at detecting faults in glass.

READING PASSAGE 2

*You should spend about 20 minutes on **Questions 14–26**, which are based on Reading Passage 2 on the following pages.*

Questions 14–17

Reading Passage 2 has six paragraphs, **A–F**.

*Choose the correct heading for paragraphs **B** and **D–F** from the list of headings below.*

*Write the correct number, **i–ix**, in boxes 14–17 on your answer sheet.*

List of Headings
i   Predicting climatic changes
ii   The relevance of the Little Ice Age today
iii How cities contribute to climate change
iv   Human impact on the climate
v   How past climatic conditions can be determined
vi   A growing need for weather records
vii A study covering a thousand years
viii People have always responded to climate change
ix   Enough food at last

Example	*Answer*
Paragraph **A**	**viii**

14   Paragraph **B**

Example	*Answer*
Paragraph **C**	**v**

15   Paragraph **D**

16   Paragraph **E**

17   Paragraph **F**

THE LITTLE ICE AGE

A This book will provide a detailed examination of the Little Ice Age and other climatic shifts, but, before I embark on that, let me provide a historical context. We tend to think of climate – as opposed to weather – as something unchanging, yet humanity has been at the mercy of climate change for its entire existence, with at least eight glacial episodes in the past 730,000 years. Our ancestors adapted to the universal but irregular global warming since the end of the last great Ice Age, around 10,000 years ago, with dazzling opportunism. They developed strategies for surviving harsh drought cycles, decades of heavy rainfall or unaccustomed cold; adopted agriculture and stock-raising, which revolutionised human life; and founded the world's first pre-industrial civilisations in Egypt, Mesopotamia and the Americas. But the price of sudden climate change, in famine, disease and suffering, was often high.

B The Little Ice Age lasted from roughly 1300 until the middle of the nineteenth century. Only two centuries ago, Europe experienced a cycle of bitterly cold winters; mountain glaciers in the Swiss Alps were the lowest in recorded memory, and pack ice surrounded Iceland for much of the year. The climatic events of the Little Ice Age did more than help shape the modern world. They are the deeply important context for the current unprecedented global warming. The Little Ice Age was far from a deep freeze, however; rather an irregular seesaw of rapid climatic shifts, few lasting more than a quarter-century, driven by complex and still little understood interactions between the atmosphere and the ocean. The seesaw brought cycles of intensely cold winters and easterly winds, then switched abruptly to years of heavy spring and early summer rains, mild winters, and frequent Atlantic storms, or to periods of droughts, light northeasterly winds, and summer heat waves.

C Reconstructing the climate changes of the past is extremely difficult, because systematic weather observations began only a few centuries ago, in Europe and North America. Records from India and tropical Africa are even more recent. For the time before records began, we have only 'proxy records' reconstructed largely from tree rings and ice cores, supplemented by a few incomplete written accounts. We now have hundreds of tree-ring records from throughout the northern hemisphere, and many from south of the equator, too, amplified with a growing body of temperature data from ice cores drilled in Antarctica, Greenland, the Peruvian Andes, and other locations. We are close to a knowledge of annual summer and winter temperature variations over much of the northern hemisphere going back 600 years.

D This book is a narrative history of climatic shifts during the past ten centuries, and some of the ways in which people in Europe adapted to them. Part One describes the Medieval Warm Period, roughly 900 to 1200. During these three centuries, Norse voyagers from Northern Europe explored northern seas, settled Greenland, and visited North America. It was not a time of uniform warmth, for then, as always since the Great Ice Age, there were constant shifts in rainfall and temperature. Mean European temperatures were about the same as today, perhaps slightly cooler.

E It is known that the Little Ice Age cooling began in Greenland and the Arctic in about 1200. As the Arctic ice pack spread southward, Norse voyages to the west were rerouted into the open Atlantic, then ended altogether. Storminess increased in the North Atlantic and North Sea. Colder, much wetter weather descended on Europe between 1315 and 1319, when thousands perished in a continent-wide famine. By 1400, the weather had become decidedly more unpredictable and stormier, with sudden shifts and lower temperatures that culminated in the cold decades of the late sixteenth century. Fish were a vital commodity in growing towns and cities, where food supplies were a constant concern. Dried cod and herring were already the staples of the European fish trade, but changes in water temperatures forced fishing fleets to work further offshore. The Basques, Dutch, and English developed the first offshore fishing boats adapted to a colder and stormier Atlantic. A gradual agricultural revolution in northern Europe stemmed from concerns over food supplies at a time of rising populations. The revolution involved intensive commercial farming and the growing of animal fodder on land not previously used for crops. The increased productivity from farmland made some countries self-sufficient in grain and livestock and offered effective protection against famine.

F Global temperatures began to rise slowly after 1850, with the beginning of the Modern Warm Period. There was a vast migration from Europe by land-hungry farmers and others, to which the famine caused by the Irish potato blight contributed, to North America, Australia, New Zealand, and southern Africa. Millions of hectares of forest and woodland fell before the newcomers' axes between 1850 and 1890, as intensive European farming methods expanded across the world. The unprecedented land clearance released vast quantities of carbon dioxide into the atmosphere, triggering for the first time humanly caused global warming. Temperatures climbed more rapidly in the twentieth century as the use of fossil fuels proliferated and greenhouse gas levels continued to soar. The rise has been even steeper since the early 1980s. The Little Ice Age has given way to a new climatic regime, marked by prolonged and steady warming. At the same time, extreme weather events like Category 5 hurricanes are becoming more frequent.

Questions 18–22

*Complete the summary using the list of words, **A–I**, below.*

*Write the correct letter, **A–I**, in boxes 18–22 on your answer sheet.*

Weather during the Little Ice Age

Documentation of past weather conditions is limited: our main sources of knowledge of conditions in the distant past are **18** .... and **19** .... We can deduce that the Little Ice Age was a time of **20** .... , rather than of consistent freezing. Within it there were some periods of very cold winters, others of **21** .... and heavy rain, and yet others that saw **22** .... with no rain at all.

A	climatic shifts	**B**	ice cores	**C**	tree rings
D	glaciers	**E**	interactions	**F**	weather observations
G	heat waves	**H**	storms	**I**	written accounts

Questions 23–26

Classify the following events as occurring during the

    A   *Medieval Warm Period*
    B   *Little Ice Age*
    C   *Modern Warm Period*

*Write the correct letter, **A**, **B** or **C**, in boxes 23–26 on your answer sheet.*

23   Many Europeans started farming abroad.

24   The cutting down of trees began to affect the climate.

25   Europeans discovered other lands.

26   Changes took place in fishing patterns.

READING PASSAGE 3

You should spend about 20 minutes on **Questions 27–40**, which are based on Reading Passage 3 on the following pages.

Questions 27–32

Reading Passage 3 has six paragraphs, **A–F**.

Choose the correct heading for each paragraph from the list of headings below.

Write the correct number, **i–viii**, in boxes 27–32 on your answer sheet.

List of Headings

i	The difficulties of talking about smells
ii	The role of smell in personal relationships
iii	Future studies into smell
iv	The relationship between the brain and the nose
v	The interpretation of smells as a factor in defining groups
vi	Why our sense of smell is not appreciated
vii	Smell is our superior sense
viii	The relationship between smell and feelings

---

27 Paragraph **A**

28 Paragraph **B**

29 Paragraph **C**

30 Paragraph **D**

31 Paragraph **E**

32 Paragraph **F**

The meaning and power of smell

The sense of smell, or olfaction, is powerful. Odours affect us on a physical, psychological and social level. For the most part, however, we breathe in the aromas which surround us without being consciously aware of their importance to us. It is only when the faculty of smell is impaired for some reason that we begin to realise the essential role the sense of smell plays in our sense of well-being

A A survey conducted by Anthony Synott at Montreal's Concordia University asked participants to comment on how important smell was to them in their lives. It became apparent that smell can evoke strong emotional responses. A scent associated with a good experience can bring a rush of joy, while a foul odour or one associated with a bad memory may make us grimace with disgust. Respondents to the survey noted that many of their olfactory likes and dislikes were based on emotional associations. Such associations can be powerful enough so that odours that we would generally label unpleasant become agreeable, and those that we would generally consider fragrant become disagreeable for particular individuals. The perception of smell, therefore, consists not only of the sensation of the odours themselves, but of the experiences and emotions associated with them.

B Odours are also essential cues in social bonding. One respondent to the survey believed that there is no true emotional bonding without touching and smelling a loved one. In fact, infants recognise the odours of their mothers soon after birth and adults can often identify their children or spouses by scent. In one well-known test, women and men were able to distinguish by smell alone clothing worn by their marriage partners from similar clothing worn by other people. Most of the subjects would probably never have given much thought to odour as a cue for identifying family members before being involved in the test, but as the experiment revealed, even when not consciously considered, smells register.

C In spite of its importance to our emotional and sensory lives, smell is probably the most undervalued sense in many cultures. The reason often given for the low regard in which smell is held is that, in comparison with its importance among animals, the human sense of smell is feeble and undeveloped. While it is true that the olfactory powers of humans are nothing like as fine as those possessed by certain animals, they are still remarkably acute. Our noses are able to recognise thousands of smells, and to perceive odours which are present only in extremely small quantities.

D Smell, however, is a highly elusive phenomenon. Odours, unlike colours, for instance, cannot be named in many languages because the specific vocabulary simply doesn't exist. 'It smells like . . . ,' we have to say when describing an odour, struggling to express our olfactory experience. Nor can odours be recorded: there is no effective way to either capture or store them over time. In the realm of olfaction, we must make do with descriptions and recollections. This has implications for olfactory research.

E   Most of the research on smell undertaken to date has been of a physical scientific nature. Significant advances have been made in the understanding of the biological and chemical nature of olfaction, but many fundamental questions have yet to be answered. Researchers have still to decide whether smell is one sense or two – one responding to odours proper and the other registering odourless chemicals in the air. Other unanswered questions are whether the nose is the only part of the body affected by odours, and how smells can be measured objectively given the non-physical components. Questions like these mean that interest in the psychology of smell is inevitably set to play an increasingly important role for researchers.

F   However, smell is not simply a biological and psychological phenomenon. Smell is cultural, hence it is a social and historical phenomenon. Odours are invested with cultural values: smells that are considered to be offensive in some cultures may be perfectly acceptable in others. Therefore, our sense of smell is a means of, and model for, interacting with the world. Different smells can provide us with intimate and emotionally charged experiences and the value that we attach to these experiences is interiorised by the members of society in a deeply personal way. Importantly, our commonly held feelings about smells can help distinguish us from other cultures. The study of the cultural history of smell is, therefore, in a very real sense, an investigation into the essence of human culture.

Questions 33–36

*Choose the correct letter, **A, B, C** or **D**.*

Write the correct letter in boxes 33–36 on your answer sheet.

33   According to the introduction, we become aware of the importance of smell when

   A   we discover a new smell.
   B   we experience a powerful smell.
   C   our ability to smell is damaged.
   D   we are surrounded by odours.

34   The experiment described in paragraph B

   A   shows how we make use of smell without realising it.
   B   demonstrates that family members have a similar smell.
   C   proves that a sense of smell is learnt.
   D   compares the sense of smell in males and females.

35 What is the writer doing in paragraph C?

    A   supporting other research
    B   making a proposal
    C   rejecting a common belief
    D   describing limitations

36 What does the writer suggest about the study of smell in the atmosphere in paragraph E?

    A   The measurement of smell is becoming more accurate.
    B   Researchers believe smell is a purely physical reaction.
    C   Most smells are inoffensive.
    D   Smell is yet to be defined.

Questions 37–40

Complete the sentences below.

*Choose **ONE WORD ONLY** from the passage for each answer.*

Write your answers in boxes 37–40 on your answer sheet.

37 Tests have shown that odours can help people recognise the .... belonging to their husbands and wives.

38 Certain linguistic groups may have difficulty describing smell because they lack the appropriate ....

39 The sense of smell may involve response to .... which do not smell, in addition to obvious odours.

40 Odours regarded as unpleasant in certain .... are not regarded as unpleasant in others.

WRITING

WRITING TASK 1

You should spend about 20 minutes on this task.

The three pie charts below show the changes in annual spending by a particular UK school in 1981, 1991 and 2001.

Summarise the information by selecting and reporting the main features, and make comparisons where relevant.

Write at least 150 words.

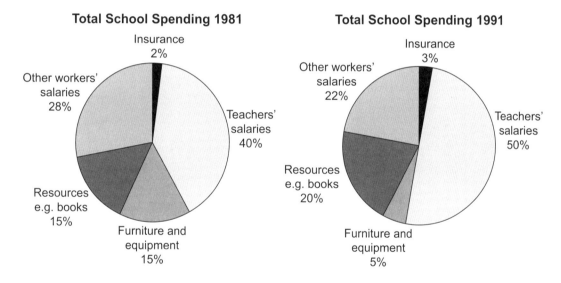

Total School Spending 1981

Total School Spending 1991

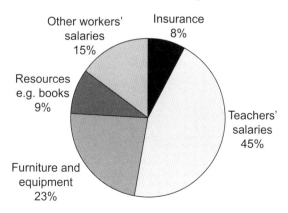

Total School Spending 2001

WRITING TASK 2

You should spend about 40 minutes on this task.

Write about the following topic:

> **Nowadays the way many people interact with each other has changed because of technology.**
>
> **In what ways has technology affected the types of relationships people make?**
>
> **Has this become a positive or negative development?**

Give reasons for your answer and include any relevant examples from your own knowledge or experience.

Write at least 250 words.

SPEAKING

PART 1

The examiner asks the candidate about him/herself, his/her home, work or studies and other familiar topics.

EXAMPLE

Newspapers and Magazines

- Which magazines and newspapers do you read? [Why?]
- What kinds of article are you most interested in? [Why?]
- Have you ever read a newspaper or magazine in a foreign language? [When/Why?]
- Do you think reading a newspaper or magazine in a foreign language is a good way to learn the language? [Why/Why not?]

PART 2

> **Describe a restaurant that you enjoyed going to.**
>
> **You should say:**
>   **where the restaurant was**
>   **why you chose this restaurant**
>   **what type of food you ate in this restaurant and**
> **explain why you enjoyed eating in this restaurant.**

You will have to talk about the topic for one to two minutes. You have one minute to think about what you are going to say.
You can make some notes to help you if you wish.

PART 3

Discussion topics:

Restaurants

Example questions:
Why do you think people go to restaurants when they want to celebrate something?
Which are more popular in your country: fast food restaurants or traditional restaurants? Why do you think that is?
Some people say that food in an expensive restaurant is always better than food in a cheap restaurant – would you agree?

Producing food

Example questions:
Do you think there will be a greater choice of food available in shops in the future, or will there be less choice?
What effects has modern technology had on the way food is produced?
How important is it for a country to be able to grow all the food it needs, without importing any from other countries?

Test 3

PART 1   Questions 1–10

Questions 1–3

Complete the form below.

Write ONE WORD AND/OR A NUMBER for each answer.

Rented Properties Customer's Requirements	
Name:	Steven Godfrey
No. of bedrooms:	four
Preferred location:	in the **1** .... area of town
Maximum monthly rent:	**2** £ ....
Length of let required:	**3** ....
Starting:	September 1st

Questions 4–8

Complete the table below.

*Write **ONE WORD AND/OR A NUMBER** for each answer.*

Address	Rooms	Monthly rent	Problem
Oakington Avenue	living/dining room, separate kitchen	£550	no **4** ....
Mead Street	large living room and kitchen, bathroom and a cloakroom	£580	the **5** .... is too large
Hamilton Road	living room, kitchen-diner, and a **6**	£550	too **7** ....
Devon Close	living room, dining room, small kitchen	**8** £	none

Questions 9 and 10

*Choose **TWO** letters, **A–E**.*

Which **TWO** facilities in the district of Devon Close are open to the public at the moment?

    A   museum
    B   concert hall
    C   cinema
    D   sports centre
    E   swimming pool

PART 2   *Questions 11–20*

Questions 11–16

Complete the notes below.

Write **NO MORE THAN TWO WORDS AND/OR A NUMBER** *for each answer.*

THE NATIONAL ARTS CENTRE

Well known for:	**11** ....
Complex consists of:	concert rooms
	theatres
	cinemas
	art galleries
	public library
	restaurants
	a **12** ....
Historical background:	1940 – area destroyed by bombs
	1960s–1970s – Centre was **13** .... and built
	in **14** .... – opened to public
Managed by:	the **15** ....
Open:	**16** .... days per year

Questions 17–20

Complete the table below.

Write **NO MORE THAN THREE WORDS AND/OR A NUMBER** *for each answer.*

Day	Time	Event	Venue	Ticket price
Monday and Tuesday	7.30 p.m.	'The Magic Flute' (opera by Mozart)	**17**	from £8.00
Wednesday	8.00 p.m.	**18** '.......................' (Canadian film)	Cinema 2	**19** £ ....
Saturday and Sunday	11 a.m. to 10 p.m.	**20** '.......................' (art exhibition)	Gallery 1	free

PART 3   *Questions 21–30*

Questions 21–26

*Choose the correct letter, **A**, **B** or **C**.*

Latin American studies

21 Paul decided to get work experience in South America because he wanted

    A   to teach English there.
    B   to improve his Spanish.
    C   to learn about Latin American life.

22 What project work did Paul originally intend to get involved in?

    A   construction
    B   agriculture
    C   tourism

23 Why did Paul change from one project to another?

    A   His first job was not well organised.
    B   He found doing the routine work very boring.
    C   The work was too physically demanding.

24 In the village community, he learnt how important it was to

    A   respect family life.
    B   develop trust.
    C   use money wisely.

25 What does Paul say about his project manager?

    A   He let Paul do most of the work.
    B   His plans were too ambitious.
    C   He was very supportive of Paul.

26 Paul was surprised to be given

    A   a computer to use.
    B   so little money to live on.
    C   an extension to his contract.

Questions 27–30

What does Paul decide about each of the following modules?

*Write the correct letter, **A**, **B** or **C**, next to questions 27–30.*

A	He will do this.
B	He might do this.
C	He won't do this.

Module

27   Gender Studies in Latin America   ....

28   Second Language Acquisition   ....

29   Indigenous Women's Lives   ....

30   Portuguese Language Studies   ....

PART 4   *Questions 31–40*

Questions 31–34

*Choose the correct letter, **A**, **B** or **C**.*

Trying to repeat success

31 Compared to introducing new business processes, attempts to copy existing processes are

A   more attractive.
B   more frequent.
C   more straightforward.

32 Most research into the repetition of success in business has

A   been done outside the United States.
B   produced consistent findings.
C   related to only a few contexts.

33 What does the speaker say about consulting experts?

A   Too few managers ever do it.
B   It can be useful in certain circumstances.
C   Experts are sometimes unwilling to give advice.

34 An expert's knowledge about a business system may be incomplete because

A   some details are difficult for workers to explain.
B   workers choose not to mention certain details.
C   details are sometimes altered by workers.

Questions 35–40

Complete the notes below.

*Write **ONE WORD ONLY** for each answer.*

Setting up systems based on an existing process

Two mistakes

Manager tries to:

- improve on the original process
- create an ideal **35** .... from the best parts of several processes

Cause of problems

- information was inaccurate
- comparison between the business settings was invalid
- disadvantages were overlooked, e.g. effect of changes on **36** ....

Solution

- change **37** ....
- impose rigorous **38** ....
- copy original very closely:
  - physical features of the **39** ....
  - the **40** .... of original employees

---

READING

READING PASSAGE 1

*You should spend about 20 minutes on **Questions 1–13** which are based on Reading Passage 1 below.*

Striking Back at Lightning With Lasers

Seldom is the weather more dramatic than when thunderstorms strike. Their electrical fury inflicts death or serious injury on around 500 people each year in the United States alone. As the clouds roll in, a leisurely round of golf can become a terrifying dice with death – out in the open, a lone golfer may be a lightning bolt's most inviting target. And there is damage to property too. Lightning damage costs American power companies more than $100 million a year.

But researchers in the United States and Japan are planning to hit back. Already in laboratory trials they have tested strategies for neutralising the power of thunderstorms, and this winter they will brave real storms, equipped with an armoury of lasers that they will be pointing towards the heavens to discharge thunderclouds before lightning can strike.

The idea of forcing storm clouds to discharge their lightning on command is not new. In the early 1960s, researchers tried firing rockets trailing wires into thunderclouds to set up an easy discharge path for the huge electric charges that these clouds generate. The technique survives to this day at a test site in Florida run by the University of Florida, with support from the Electrical Power Research Institute (EPRI), based in California. EPRI, which is funded by power companies, is looking at ways to protect the United States' power grid from lightning strikes. 'We can cause the lightning to strike where we want it to using rockets,' says Ralph Bernstein, manager of lightning projects at EPRI. The rocket site is providing precise measurements of lightning voltages and allowing engineers to check how electrical equipment bears up.

Bad behaviour

But while rockets are fine for research, they cannot provide the protection from lightning strikes that everyone is looking for. The rockets cost around $1,200 each, can only be fired at a limited frequency and their failure rate is about 40 per cent. And even when they do trigger lightning, things still do not always go according to plan. 'Lightning is not perfectly well behaved,' says Bernstein. 'Occasionally, it will take a branch and go someplace it wasn't supposed to go.'

And anyway, who would want to fire streams of rockets in a populated area? 'What goes up must come down,' points out Jean-Claude Diels of the University of New Mexico. Diels is leading a project, which is backed by EPRI, to try to use lasers to discharge lightning safely

– and safety is a basic requirement since no one wants to put themselves or their expensive equipment at risk. With around $500,000 invested so far, a promising system is just emerging from the laboratory.

The idea began some 20 years ago, when high-powered lasers were revealing their ability to extract electrons out of atoms and create ions. If a laser could generate a line of ionisation in the air all the way up to a storm cloud, this conducting path could be used to guide lightning to Earth, before the electric field becomes strong enough to break down the air in an uncontrollable surge. To stop the laser itself being struck, it would not be pointed straight at the clouds. Instead it would be directed at a mirror, and from there into the sky. The mirror would be protected by placing lightning conductors close by. Ideally, the cloud-zapper (gun) would be cheap enough to be installed around all key power installations, and portable enough to be taken to international sporting events to beam up at brewing storm clouds.

A stumbling block

However, there is still a big stumbling block. The laser is no nifty portable: it's a monster that takes up a whole room. Diels is trying to cut down the size and says that a laser around the size of a small table is in the offing. He plans to test this more manageable system on live thunderclouds next summer.

Bernstein says that Diels's system is attracting lots of interest from the power companies. But they have not yet come up with the $5 million that EPRI says will be needed to develop a commercial system, by making the lasers yet smaller and cheaper. 'I cannot say I have money yet, but I'm working on it,' says Bernstein. He reckons that the forthcoming field tests will be the turning point – and he's hoping for good news. Bernstein predicts 'an avalanche of interest and support' if all goes well. He expects to see cloud-zappers eventually costing $50,000 to $100,000 each.

Other scientists could also benefit. With a lightning 'switch' at their fingertips, materials scientists could find out what happens when mighty currents meet matter. Diels also hopes to see the birth of 'interactive meteorology' – not just forecasting the weather but controlling it. 'If we could discharge clouds, we might affect the weather,' he says.

And perhaps, says Diels, we'll be able to confront some other meteorological menaces. 'We think we could prevent hail by inducing lightning,' he says. Thunder, the shock wave that comes from a lightning flash, is thought to be the trigger for the torrential rain that is typical of storms. A laser thunder factory could shake the moisture out of clouds, perhaps preventing the formation of the giant hailstones that threaten crops. With luck, as the storm clouds gather this winter, laser-toting researchers could, for the first time, strike back.

Questions 1–3

*Choose the correct letter, **A**, **B**, **C** or **D**.*

Write the correct letter in boxes 1–3 on your answer sheet.

1   The main topic discussed in the text is

    A   the damage caused to US golf courses and golf players by lightning strikes.
    B   the effect of lightning on power supplies in the US and in Japan.
    C   a variety of methods used in trying to control lightning strikes.
    D   a laser technique used in trying to control lightning strikes.

2   According to the text, every year lightning

    A   does considerable damage to buildings during thunderstorms.
    B   kills or injures mainly golfers in the United States.
    C   kills or injures around 500 people throughout the world.
    D   damages more than 100 American power companies.

3   Researchers at the University of Florida and at the University of New Mexico

    A   receive funds from the same source.
    B   are using the same techniques.
    C   are employed by commercial companies.
    D   are in opposition to each other.

Questions 4–6

Complete the sentences below.

*Choose **NO MORE THAN TWO WORDS** from the passage for each answer.*

Write your answers in boxes 4–6 on your answer sheet.

4   EPRI receives financial support from ....

5   The advantage of the technique being developed by Diels is that it can be
    used ....

6   The main difficulty associated with using the laser equipment is related to
    its ....

Questions 7–10

*Complete the summary using the list of words, **A–I**, below.*

*Write the correct letter, **A–I**, in boxes 7–10 on your answer sheet.*

In this method, a laser is used to create a line of ionisation by removing electrons from **7** .... This laser is then directed at **8** .... in order to control electrical charges, a method which is less dangerous than using **9** .... As a protection for the lasers, the beams are aimed firstly at **10** ....

A	cloud-zappers	**B**	atoms	**C**	storm clouds
D	mirrors	**E**	technique	**F**	ions
G	rockets	**H**	conductors	**I**	thunder

Questions 11–13

Do the following statements agree with the information given in Reading Passage 1?

In boxes 11–13 on your answer sheet write

> **YES**   *if the statement agrees with the claims of the writer*
> **NO**   *if the statement contradicts the claims of the writer*
> **NOT GIVEN**   *if it is impossible to say what the writer thinks about this*

11 Power companies have given Diels enough money to develop his laser.

12 Obtaining money to improve the lasers will depend on tests in real storms.

13 Weather forecasters are intensely interested in Diels's system.

READING PASSAGE 2

*You should spend about 20 minutes on **Questions 14–26**, which are based on Reading Passage 2 below.*

The Nature of Genius

There has always been an interest in geniuses and prodigies. The word 'genius', from the Latin *gens* (= family) and the term 'genius', meaning 'begetter', comes from the early Roman cult of a divinity as the head of the family. In its earliest form, genius was concerned with the ability of the head of the family, the *paterfamilias*, to perpetuate himself. Gradually, genius came to represent a person's characteristics and thence an individual's highest attributes derived from his 'genius' or guiding spirit. Today, people still look to stars or genes, astrology or genetics, in the hope of finding the source of exceptional abilities or personal characteristics.

The concept of genius and of gifts has become part of our folk culture, and attitudes are ambivalent towards them. We envy the gifted and mistrust them. In the mythology of giftedness, it is popularly believed that if people are talented in one area, they must be defective in another, that intellectuals are impractical, that prodigies burn too brightly too soon and burn out, that gifted people are eccentric, that they are physical weaklings, that there's a thin line between genius and madness, that genius runs in families, that the gifted are so clever they don't need special help, that giftedness is the same as having a high IQ, that some races are more intelligent or musical or mathematical than others, that genius goes unrecognised and unrewarded, that adversity makes men wise or that people with gifts have a responsibility to use them. Language has been enriched with such terms as 'highbrow', 'egghead', 'blue-stocking', 'wiseacre', 'know-all', 'boffin' and, for many, 'intellectual' is a term of denigration.

The nineteenth century saw considerable interest in the nature of genius, and produced not a few studies of famous prodigies. Perhaps for us today, two of the most significant aspects of most of these studies of genius are the frequency with which early encouragement and teaching by parents and tutors had beneficial effects on the intellectual, artistic or musical development of the children but caused great difficulties of adjustment later in their lives, and the frequency with which abilities went unrecognised by teachers and schools. However, the difficulty with the evidence produced by these studies, fascinating as they are in collecting together anecdotes and apparent similarities and exceptions, is that they are not what we would today call norm-referenced. In other words, when, for instance, information is collated about early illnesses, methods of upbringing, schooling, etc., we must also take into account information from other historical sources about how common or exceptional these were at the time. For instance, infant mortality was high and life expectancy much shorter than today, home tutoring was common in the families of the nobility and wealthy, bullying and corporal punishment were common at the best independent schools and, for the most part, the cases studied were members of the privileged classes. It was only with the growth of paediatrics and psychology in the twentieth century that studies could be carried out on a more objective, if still not always very scientific, basis.

Geniuses, however they are defined, are but the peaks which stand out through the mist of history and are visible to the particular observer from his or her particular vantage point. Change the observers and the vantage points, clear away some of the mist, and a different lot of peaks appear. Genius is a term we apply to those whom we recognise for their outstanding achievements and who stand near the end of the continuum of human abilities which reaches back through the mundane and mediocre to the incapable. There is still much truth in Dr Samuel Johnson's observation, 'The true genius is a mind of large general powers, accidentally determined to some particular direction'. We may disagree with the 'general', for we doubt if all musicians of genius could have become scientists of genius or vice versa, but there is no doubting the accidental determination which nurtured or triggered their gifts into those channels into which they have poured their powers so successfully. Along the continuum of abilities are hundreds of thousands of gifted men and women, boys and girls.

What we appreciate, enjoy or marvel at in the works of genius or the achievements of prodigies are the manifestations of skills or abilities which are similar to, but so much superior to, our own. But that their minds are not different from our own is demonstrated by the fact that the hard-won discoveries of scientists like Kepler or Einstein become the commonplace knowledge of schoolchildren and the once outrageous shapes and colours of an artist like Paul Klee so soon appear on the fabrics we wear. This does not minimise the supremacy of their achievements, which outstrip our own as the sub-four-minute milers outstrip our jogging.

To think of geniuses and the gifted as having uniquely different brains is only reasonable if we accept that each human brain is uniquely different. The purpose of instruction is to make us even more different from one another, and in the process of being educated we can learn from the achievements of those more gifted than ourselves. But before we try to emulate geniuses or encourage our children to do so we should note that some of the things we learn from them may prove unpalatable. We may envy their achievements and fame, but we should also recognise the price they may have paid in terms of perseverance, single-mindedness, dedication, restrictions on their personal lives, the demands upon their energies and time, and how often they had to display great courage to preserve their integrity or to make their way to the top.

Genius and giftedness are relative descriptive terms of no real substance. We may, at best, give them some precision by defining them and placing them in a context but, whatever we do, we should never delude ourselves into believing that gifted children or geniuses are different from the rest of humanity, save in the degree to which they have developed the performance of their abilities.

Questions 14–18

*Choose **FIVE** letters, **A–K**.*

Write the correct letters in boxes 14–18 on your answer sheet.

NB　　*Your answers may be given in any order.*

Below are listed some popular beliefs about genius and giftedness.

Which **FIVE** of these beliefs are reported by the writer of the text?

A	Truly gifted people are talented in all areas.
B	The talents of geniuses are soon exhausted.
C	Gifted people should use their gifts.
D	A genius appears once in every generation.
E	Genius can be easily destroyed by discouragement.
F	Genius is inherited.
G	Gifted people are very hard to live with.
H	People never appreciate true genius.
I	Geniuses are natural leaders.
J	Gifted people develop their greatness through difficulties.
K	Genius will always reveal itself.

Questions 19–26

Do the following statements agree with the information given in Reading Passage 2?

In boxes 19–26 on your answer sheet, write

TRUE	*if the statement agrees with the information*
FALSE	*if the statement contradicts the information*
NOT GIVEN	*if there is no information on this*

19   Nineteenth-century studies of the nature of genius failed to take into account the uniqueness of the person's upbringing.

20   Nineteenth-century studies of genius lacked both objectivity and a proper scientific approach.

21   A true genius has general powers capable of excellence in any area.

22   The skills of ordinary individuals are in essence the same as the skills of prodigies.

23   The ease with which truly great ideas are accepted and taken for granted fails to lessen their significance.

24   Giftedness and genius deserve proper scientific research into their true nature so that all talent may be retained for the human race.

25   Geniuses often pay a high price to achieve greatness.

26   To be a genius is worth the high personal cost.

READING PASSAGE 3

*You should spend about 20 minutes on **Questions 27–40**, which are based on Reading Passage 3 on the following pages.*

Questions 27–32

Reading Passage 3 has seven paragraphs, **A–G**.

*Choose the correct heading for paragraphs **B–G** from the list of headings below.*

*Write the correct number, **i–x**, in boxes 27–32 on your answer sheet.*

List of Headings

i	The biological clock
ii	Why dying is beneficial
iii	The ageing process of men and women
iv	Prolonging your life
v	Limitations of life span
vi	Modes of development of different species
vii	A stable life span despite improvements
viii	Energy consumption
ix	Fundamental differences in ageing of objects and organisms
x	Repair of genetic material

Example	*Answer*
Paragraph **A**	**v**

---

27 Paragraph **B**

28 Paragraph **C**

29 Paragraph **D**

30 Paragraph **E**

31 Paragraph **F**

32 Paragraph **G**

HOW DOES THE BIOLOGICAL CLOCK TICK?

A   Our life span is restricted. Everyone accepts this as 'biologically' obvious. 'Nothing lives for ever!' However, in this statement we think of artificially produced, technical objects, products which are subjected to natural wear and tear during use. This leads to the result that at some time or other the object stops working and is unusable ('death' in the biological sense). But are the wear and tear and loss of function of technical objects and the death of living organisms really similar or comparable?

B   Our 'dead' products are 'static', closed systems. It is always the basic material which constitutes the object and which, in the natural course of things, is worn down and becomes 'older'. Ageing in this case must occur according to the laws of physical chemistry and of thermodynamics. Although the same law holds for a living organism, the result of this law is not inexorable in the same way. At least as long as a biological system has the ability to renew itself it could actually become older without ageing; an organism is an open, dynamic system through which new material continuously flows. Destruction of old material and formation of new material are thus in permanent dynamic equilibrium. The material of which the organism is formed changes continuously. Thus our bodies continuously exchange old substance for new, just like a spring which more or less maintains its form and movement, but in which the water molecules are always different.

C   Thus ageing and death should not be seen as inevitable, particularly as the organism possesses many mechanisms for repair. It is not, in principle, necessary for a biological system to age and die. Nevertheless, a restricted life span, ageing, and then death are basic characteristics of life. The reason for this is easy to recognise: in nature, the existent organisms either adapt or are regularly replaced by new types. Because of changes in the genetic material (mutations) these have new characteristics and in the course of their individual lives they are tested for optimal or better adaptation to the environmental conditions. Immortality would disturb this system – it needs room for new and better life. This is the basic problem of evolution.

D   Every organism has a life span which is highly characteristic. There are striking differences in life span between different species, but within one species the parameter is relatively constant. For example, the average duration of human life has hardly changed in thousands of years. Although more and more people attain an advanced age as a result of developments in medical care and better nutrition, the characteristic upper limit for most remains 80 years. A further argument against the simple wear and tear theory is the observation that the time within which organisms age lies between a few days (even a few hours for unicellular organisms) and several thousand years, as with mammoth trees.

E If a life span is a genetically determined biological characteristic, it is logically necessary to propose the existence of an internal clock, which in some way measures and controls the ageing process and which finally determines death as the last step in a fixed programme. Like the life span, the metabolic rate has for different organisms a fixed mathematical relationship to the body mass. In comparison to the life span this relationship is 'inverted': the larger the organism the lower its metabolic rate. Again this relationship is valid not only for birds, but also, similarly on average within the systematic unit, for all other organisms (plants, animals, unicellular organisms).

F Animals which behave 'frugally' with energy become particularly old, for example, crocodiles and tortoises. Parrots and birds of prey are often held chained up. Thus they are not able to 'experience life' and so they attain a high life span in captivity. Animals which save energy by hibernation or lethargy (e.g. bats or hedgehogs) live much longer than those which are always active. The metabolic rate of mice can be reduced by a very low consumption of food (hunger diet). They then may live twice as long as their well fed comrades. Women become distinctly (about 10 per cent) older than men. If you examine the metabolic rates of the two sexes you establish that the higher male metabolic rate roughly accounts for the lower male life span. That means that they live life 'energetically' – more intensively, but not for as long.

G It follows from the above that sparing use of energy reserves should tend to extend life. Extreme high performance sports may lead to optimal cardiovascular performance, but they quite certainly do not prolong life. Relaxation lowers metabolic rate, as does adequate sleep and in general an equable and balanced personality. Each of us can develop his or her own 'energy saving programme' with a little self-observation, critical self-control and, above all, logical consistency. Experience will show that to live in this way not only increases the life span but is also very healthy. This final aspect should not be forgotten.

Questions 33–36

Complete the notes below.

*Choose **NO MORE THAN TWO WORDS** from the passage for each answer.*

Write your answers in boxes 33–36 on your answer sheet.

- Objects age in accordance with principles of **33** .... and of **34** ....
- Through mutations, organisms can **35** .... better to the environment
- **36** .... would pose a serious problem for the theory of evolution

Questions 37–40

Do the following statements agree with the views of the writer in Reading Passage 3?

In boxes 37–40 on your answer sheet, write

YES	*if the statement agrees with the views of the writer*
NO	*if the statement contradicts the views of the writer*
NOT GIVEN	*if it is impossible to say what the writer thinks about this*

37 The wear and tear theory applies to both artificial objects and biological systems.

38 In principle, it is possible for a biological system to become older without ageing.

39 Within seven years, about 90 per cent of a human body is replaced as new.

40 Conserving energy may help to extend a human's life.

WRITING

WRITING TASK 1

You should spend about 20 minutes on this task.

> **The diagrams below show the stages and equipment used in the cement-making process, and how cement is used to produce concrete for building purposes.**
>
> **Summarise the information by selecting and reporting the main features, and make comparisons where relevant.**

Write at least 150 words.

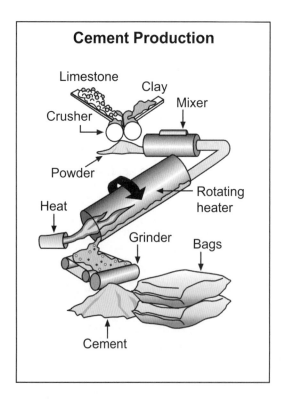

Cement Production

Limestone · Clay · Mixer · Crusher · Powder · Heat · Rotating heater · Grinder · Bags · Cement

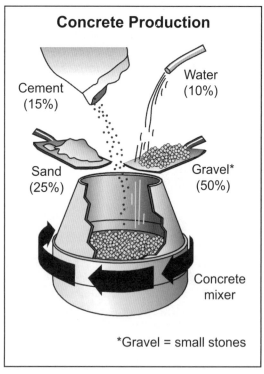

Concrete Production

Cement (15%) · Water (10%) · Sand (25%) · Gravel* (50%) · Concrete mixer

*Gravel = small stones

WRITING TASK 2

You should spend about 40 minutes on this task.

Write about the following topic:

Increasing the price of petrol is the best way to solve growing traffic and pollution problems.

To what extent do you agree or disagree?

What other measures do you think might be effective?

Give reasons for your answer and include any relevant examples from your own knowledge or experience.

Write at least 250 words.

SPEAKING

PART 1

The examiner asks the candidate about him/herself, his/her home, work or studies and other familiar topics.

EXAMPLE

Flowers

- Do you like to have flowers in your home? [Why/Why not?]
- Where would you go to buy flowers? [Why?]
- On what occasions would you give someone flowers?
- Are flowers important in your culture? [Why/Why not?]

PART 2

Describe a meeting you remember going to at work, college or school.

You should say:
  when and where the meeting was held
  who was at the meeting
  what the people at the meeting talked about and explain why you remember going to this meeting.

You will have to talk about the topic for one to two minutes.
You have one minute to think about what you are going to say.
You can make some notes to help you if you wish.

PART 3

Discussion topics:

Going to meetings

Example questions:
What are the different types of meeting that people often go to?
Some people say that no-one likes to go to meetings – what do you think?
Why can it sometimes be important to go to meetings?

International meetings

Example questions:
Why do you think world leaders often have meetings together?
What possible difficulties might be involved in organising meetings between world leaders?
Do you think that meetings between international leaders will become more frequent in the future? Or will there be less need for world leaders to meet?

Test 4

PART 1   *Questions 1–10*

Complete the notes below.

*Write **NO MORE THAN TWO WORDS AND/OR A NUMBER** for each answer.*

West Bay Hotel – details of job

- Newspaper advert for temporary staff

- Vacancies for **1** ....

- Two shifts

- Can choose your **2** .... (must be the same each week)

- Pay: £5.50 per hour, including a **3** ....

- A **4** .... is provided in the hotel

- Total weekly pay: £231

- Dress: a white shirt and **5** .... trousers (not supplied)

  a **6** .... (supplied)

- Starting date: **7** ....

- Call Jane **8** .... (Service Manager) before **9** .... tomorrow (Tel: 832009)

- She'll require a **10** ....

PART 2   *Questions 11–20*

Questions 11–13

Choose the correct letter, A, B or C.

Improvements to Red Hill Suburb

11   Community groups are mainly concerned about

    A   pedestrian safety.
    B   traffic jams.
    C   increased pollution.

12   It has been decided that the overhead power lines will be

    A   extended.
    B   buried.
    C   repaired.

13   The expenses related to the power lines will be paid for by

    A   the council.
    B   the power company.
    C   local businesses.

Questions 14–20

Label the map below.

*Write the correct letter, **A–H**, next to questions 14–20.*

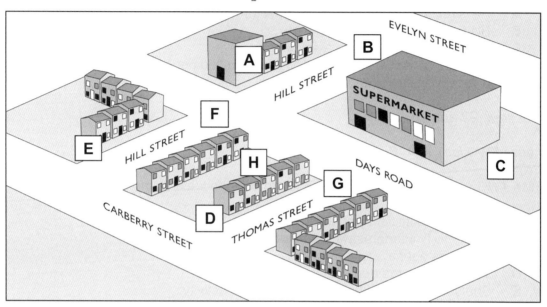

Red Hill Improvement Plan

14	trees	....
15	wider footpaths	....
16	coloured road surface	....
17	new sign	....
18	traffic lights	....
19	artwork	....
20	children's playground	....

PART 3   *Questions 21–30*

Questions 21 and 22

*Choose **TWO** letters, **A–E**.*

In which **TWO** ways is Dan financing his course?

- **A**   He is receiving money from the government.
- **B**   His family are willing to help him.
- **C**   The college is giving him a small grant.
- **D**   His local council is supporting him for a limited period.
- **E**   A former employer is providing partial funding.

Questions 23 and 24

*Choose **TWO** letters, **A–E**.*

Which **TWO** reasons does Jeannie give for deciding to leave some college clubs?

- **A**   She is not sufficiently challenged.
- **B**   The activity interferes with her studies.
- **C**   She does not have enough time.
- **D**   The activity is too demanding physically.
- **E**   She does not think she is any good at the activity.

Questions 25 and 26

*Choose the correct letter, **A**, **B** or **C**.*

25 What does Dan say about the seminars on the course?

- **A**   The other students do not give him a chance to speak.
- **B**   The seminars make him feel inferior to the other students.
- **C**   The preparation for seminars takes too much time.

26 What does Jeannie say about the tutorials on the course?

- **A**   They are an inefficient way of providing guidance.
- **B**   They are more challenging than she had expected.
- **C**   They are helping her to develop her study skills.

Questions 27–30

Complete the flow-chart below.

*Choose **NO MORE THAN TWO WORDS AND/OR A NUMBER** for each answer.*

Advice on exam preparation

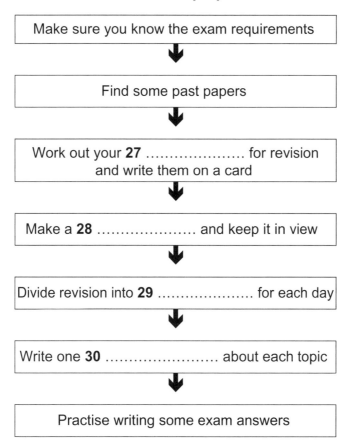

Make sure you know the exam requirements

↓

Find some past papers

↓

Work out your **27** .... for revision
and write them on a card

↓

Make a **28** .... and keep it in view

↓

Divide revision into **29** .... for each day

↓

Write one **30** .... about each topic

↓

Practise writing some exam answers

PART 4 *Questions 31–40*

Questions 31–36

Australian Aboriginal Rock Paintings

Which painting styles have the following features?

*Write the correct letter, **A**, **B** or **C**, next to questions 31–36.*

```
┌─────────────────────────────────┐
│         Painting Styles         │
│                                 │
│      A    Dynamic               │
│      B    Yam                   │
│      C    Modern                │
└─────────────────────────────────┘
```

Features

31	figures revealing bones	....
32	rounded figures	....
33	figures with parts missing	....
34	figures smaller than life size	....
35	sea creatures	....
36	plants	....

Questions 37–40

Complete the notes below.

*Write **NO MORE THAN TWO WORDS** for each answer.*

Rainbow Serpent Project

Aim of project: to identify the **37** .... used as the basis for the Rainbow Serpent

Yam Period

• environmental changes led to higher **38** ....

• traditional activities were affected, especially **39** ....

Rainbow Serpent image

• similar to a sea horse

• unusual because it appeared in inland areas

• symbolises **40** .... in Aboriginal culture

READING

READING PASSAGE 1

*You should spend about 20 minutes on **Questions 1–13**, which are based on Reading Passage 1 on the following pages.*

Questions 1–5

Reading Passage 1 has six sections, **A–F**.

*Choose the correct heading for sections **B–F** from the list of headings below.*

*Write the correct number, **i–ix**, in boxes 1–5 on your answer sheet.*

	List of Headings
i	The influence of Monbusho
ii	Helping less successful students
iii	The success of compulsory education
iv	Research findings concerning achievements in maths
v	The typical format of a maths lesson
vi	Comparative expenditure on maths education
vii	Background to middle-years education in Japan
viii	The key to Japanese successes in maths education
ix	The role of homework correction

Example	*Answer*
Section **A**	**iv**

1   Section **B**

2   Section **C**

3   Section **D**

4   Section **E**

5   Section **F**

LAND OF THE RISING SUM

A Japan has a significantly better record in terms of average mathematical attainment than England and Wales. Large sample international comparisons of pupils' attainments since the 1960s have established that not only did Japanese pupils at age 13 have better scores of average attainment, but there was also a larger proportion of 'low' attainers in England, where, incidentally, the variation in attainment scores was much greater. The percentage of Gross National Product spent on education is reasonably similar in the two countries, so how is this higher and more consistent attainment in maths achieved?

B Lower secondary schools in Japan cover three school years, from the seventh grade (age 13) to the ninth grade (age 15). Virtually all pupils at this stage attend state schools: only 3 per cent are in the private sector. Schools are usually modern in design, set well back from the road and spacious inside. Classrooms are large and pupils sit at single desks in rows. Lessons last for a standardised 50 minutes and are always followed by a 10-minute break, which gives the pupils a chance to let off steam. Teachers begin with a formal address and mutual bowing, and then concentrate on whole-class teaching.

Classes are large – usually about 40 – and are unstreamed. Pupils stay in the same class for all lessons throughout the school and develop considerable class identity and loyalty. Pupils attend the school in their own neighbourhood, which in theory removes ranking by school. In practice in Tokyo, because of the relative concentration of schools, there is some competition to get into the 'better' school in a particular area.

C Traditional ways of teaching form the basis of the lesson and the remarkably quiet classes take their own notes of the points made and the examples demonstrated. Everyone has their own copy of the textbook supplied by the central education authority, Monbusho, as part of the concept of free compulsory education up to the age of 15. These textbooks are, on the whole, small, presumably inexpensive to produce, but well set out and logically developed. (One teacher was particularly keen to introduce colour and pictures into maths textbooks: he felt this would make them more accessible to pupils brought up in a cartoon culture.) Besides approving textbooks, Monbusho also decides the highly centralised national curriculum and how it is to be delivered.

D Lessons all follow the same pattern. At the beginning, the pupils put solutions to the homework on the board, then the teachers comment, correct or elaborate as necessary. Pupils mark their own homework: this is an important principle in Japanese schooling as it enables pupils to see where and why they made a mistake, so that these can be avoided in future. No one minds mistakes or ignorance as long as you are prepared to learn from them.

After the homework has been discussed, the teacher explains the topic of the lesson, slowly and with a lot of repetition and elaboration. Examples are demonstrated on the board; questions from the textbook are worked through first with the class, and then the class is set questions from the textbook to do individually. Only rarely are supplementary worksheets distributed in a maths class. The impression is that the logical nature of the textbooks and their comprehensive coverage of different types of examples, combined with the relative homogeneity of the class, renders work sheets unnecessary. At this point, the teacher would circulate and make sure that all the pupils were coping well.

E It is remarkable that large, mixed-ability classes could be kept together for maths throughout all their compulsory schooling from 6 to 15. Teachers say that they give individual help at the end of a lesson or after school, setting extra work if necessary. In observed lessons, any strugglers would be assisted by the teacher or quietly seek help from their neighbour. Carefully fostered class identity makes pupils keen to help each other – anyway, it is in their interests since the class progresses together.

This scarcely seems adequate help to enable slow learners to keep up. However, the Japanese attitude towards education runs along the lines of 'if you work hard enough, you can do almost anything'. Parents are kept closely informed of their children's progress and will play a part in helping their children to keep up with class, sending them to 'Juku' (private evening tuition) if extra help is needed and encouraging them to work harder. It seems to work, at least for 95 per cent of the school population.

F So what are the major contributing factors in the success of maths teaching? Clearly, attitudes are important. Education is valued greatly in Japanese culture; maths is recognised as an important compulsory subject throughout schooling; and the emphasis is on hard work coupled with a focus on accuracy.

Other relevant points relate to the supportive attitude of a class towards slower pupils, the lack of competition within a class, and the positive emphasis on learning for oneself and improving one's own standard. And the view of repetitively boring lessons and learning the facts by heart, which is sometimes quoted in relation to Japanese classes, may be unfair and unjustified. No poor maths lessons were observed. They were mainly good and one or two were inspirational.

Questions 6–9

Do the following statements agree with the claims of the writer in Reading Passage 1?

In boxes 6–9 on your answer sheet, write

> **YES**   *if the statement agrees with the claims of the writer*
> **NO**   *if the statement contradicts the claims of the writer*
> **NOT GIVEN**   *if it is impossible to say what the writer thinks about this*

6 There is a wider range of achievement amongst English pupils studying maths than amongst their Japanese counterparts.

7 The percentage of Gross National Product spent on education generally reflects the level of attainment in mathematics.

8 Private schools in Japan are more modern and spacious than state-run lower secondary schools.

9 Teachers mark homework in Japanese schools.

Questions 10–13

*Choose the correct letter, **A**, **B**, **C** or **D**.*

Write the correct letter in boxes 10–13 on your answer sheet.

10 Maths textbooks in Japanese schools are

  A cheap for pupils to buy.
  B well organised and adapted to the needs of the pupils.
  C written to be used in conjunction with TV programmes.
  D not very popular with many Japanese teachers.

11 When a new maths topic is introduced,

  A students answer questions on the board.
  B students rely entirely on the textbook.
  C it is carefully and patiently explained to the students.
  D it is usual for students to use extra worksheets.

12 How do schools deal with students who experience difficulties?

  A They are given appropriate supplementary tuition.
  B They are encouraged to copy from other pupils.
  C They are forced to explain their slow progress.
  D They are placed in a mixed-ability class.

13 Why do Japanese students tend to achieve relatively high rates of success in maths?

  A It is a compulsory subject in Japan.
  B They are used to working without help from others.
  C Much effort is made and correct answers are emphasised.
  D There is a strong emphasis on repetitive learning.

READING PASSAGE 2

*You should spend about 20 minutes on **Questions 14–26**, which are based on Reading Passage 2 below.*

Biological control of pests

The continuous and reckless use of synthetic chemicals for the control of pests which pose a threat to agricultural crops and human health is proving to be counter-productive. Apart from engendering widespread ecological disorders, pesticides have contributed to the emergence of a new breed of chemical-resistant, highly lethal superbugs.

According to a recent study by the Food and Agriculture Organisation (FAO), more than 300 species of agricultural pests have developed resistance to a wide range of potent chemicals. Not to be left behind are the disease-spreading pests, about 100 species of which have become immune to a variety of insecticides now in use.

One glaring disadvantage of pesticides' application is that, while destroying harmful pests, they also wipe out many useful non-targeted organisms, which keep the growth of the pest population in check. This results in what agroecologists call the 'treadmill syndrome'. Because of their tremendous breeding potential and genetic diversity, many pests are known to withstand synthetic chemicals and bear offspring with a built-in resistance to pesticides.

The havoc that the 'treadmill syndrome' can bring about is well illustrated by what happened to cotton farmers in Central America. In the early 1940s, basking in the glory of chemical-based intensive agriculture, the farmers avidly took to pesticides as a sure measure to boost crop yield. The insecticide was applied eight times a year in the mid-1940s, rising to 28 in a season in the mid-1950s, following the sudden proliferation of three new varieties of chemical-resistant pests.

By the mid-1960s, the situation took an alarming turn with the outbreak of four more new pests, necessitating pesticide spraying to such an extent that 50% of the financial outlay on cotton production was accounted for by pesticides. In the early 1970s, the spraying frequently reached 70 times a season as the farmers were pushed to the wall by the invasion of genetically stronger insect species.

Most of the pesticides in the market today remain inadequately tested for properties that cause cancer and mutations as well as for other adverse effects on health, says a study by United States environmental agencies. The United States National Resource Defense Council has found that DDT was the most popular of a long list of dangerous chemicals in use.

In the face of the escalating perils from indiscriminate applications of pesticides, a more effective and ecologically sound strategy of biological control, involving the selective use of natural enemies of the pest population, is fast gaining popularity – though, as yet, it is a new field with limited potential. The advantage of biological control in contrast to other methods is that it provides a relatively low-cost, perpetual control system with a minimum of detrimental side-effects. When handled by experts, bio-control is safe, non-polluting and self-dispersing.

The Commonwealth Institute of Biological Control (CIBC) in Bangalore, with its global network of research laboratories and field stations, is one of the most active, non-commercial research agencies engaged in pest control by setting natural predators against parasites. CIBC also serves as a clearing-house for the export and import of biological agents for pest control world-wide.

CIBC successfully used a seed-feeding weevil, native to Mexico, to control the obnoxious parthenium weed, known to exert devious influence on agriculture and human health in both India and Australia. Similarly the Hyderabad-based Regional Research Laboratory (RRL), supported by CIBC, is now trying out an Argentinian weevil for the eradication of water hyacinth, another dangerous weed, which has become a nuisance in many parts of the world. According to Mrs Kaiser Jamil of RRL, 'The Argentinian weevil does not attack any other plant and a pair of adult bugs could destroy the weed in 4–5 days.' CIBC is also perfecting the technique for breeding parasites that prey on 'disapene scale' insects – notorious defoliants of fruit trees in the US and India.

How effectively biological control can be pressed into service is proved by the following examples. In the late 1960s, when Sri Lanka's flourishing coconut groves were plagued by leaf-mining hispides, a larval parasite imported from Singapore brought the pest under control. A natural predator indigenous to India, Neodumetia sangawani, was found useful in controlling the Rhodes grass-scale insect that was devouring forage grass in many parts of the US. By using Neochetina bruci, a beetle native to Brazil, scientists at Kerala Agricultural University freed a 12-kilometre-long canal from the clutches of the weed Salvinia molesta, popularly called 'African Payal' in Kerala. About 30,000 hectares of rice fields in Kerala are infested by this weed.

Questions 14–17

*Choose the correct letter, **A**, **B**, **C**, or **D**.*

Write the correct letter in boxes 14–17 on your answer sheet.

14   The use of pesticides has contributed to

  A   a change in the way ecologies are classified by agroecologists.
  B   an imbalance in many ecologies around the world.
  C   the prevention of ecological disasters in some parts of the world.
  D   an increase in the range of ecologies which can be usefully farmed.

15   The Food and Agriculture Organisation has counted more than 300 agricultural pests which

  A   are no longer responding to most pesticides in use.
  B   can be easily controlled through the use of pesticides.
  C   continue to spread disease in a wide range of crops.
  D   may be used as part of bio-control's replacement of pesticides.

16   Cotton farmers in Central America began to use pesticides

  A   because of an intensive government advertising campaign.
  B   in response to the appearance of new varieties of pest.
  C   as a result of changes in the seasons and the climate.
  D   to ensure more cotton was harvested from each crop.

17   By the mid-1960s, cotton farmers in Central America found that pesticides

  A   were wiping out 50% of the pests plaguing the crops.
  B   were destroying 50% of the crops they were meant to protect.
  C   were causing a 50% increase in the number of new pests reported.
  D   were costing 50% of the total amount they spent on their crops.

Questions 18–21

Do the following statements agree with the claims of the writer in Reading Passage 2?

In boxes 18–21 on your answer sheet, write

> **YES**   *if the statement agrees with the claims of the writer*
> **NO**   *if the statement contradicts the claims of the writer*
> **NOT GIVEN** *if it is impossible to say what the writer thinks about this*

18 Disease-spreading pests respond more quickly to pesticides than agricultural pests do.

19 A number of pests are now born with an innate immunity to some pesticides.

20 Biological control entails using synthetic chemicals to try and change the genetic make-up of the pests' offspring.

21 Bio-control is free from danger under certain circumstances.

Questions 22–26

*Complete each sentence with the correct ending, **A–I**, below.*

*Write the correct letter, **A–I**, in boxes 22–26 on your answer sheet.*

22 Disapene scale insects feed on

23 Neodumetia sangawani ate

24 Leaf-mining hispides blighted

25 An Argentinian weevil may be successful in wiping out

26 Salvinia molesta plagues

> **A** forage grass.
> **B** rice fields.
> **C** coconut trees.
> **D** fruit trees.
> **E** water hyacinth.
> **F** parthenium weed.
> **G** Brazilian beetles.
> **H** grass-scale insects.
> **I** larval parasites.

READING PASSAGE 3

*You should spend about 20 minutes on **Questions 27–40**, which are based on Reading Passage 3 below.*

Collecting Ant Specimens

Collecting ants can be as simple as picking up stray ones and placing them in a glass jar, or as complicated as completing an exhaustive survey of all species present in an area and estimating their relative abundances. The exact method used will depend on the final purpose of the collections. For taxonomy, or classification, long series, from a single nest, which contain all castes (workers, including majors and minors, and, if present, queens and males) are desirable, to allow the determination of variation within species. For ecological studies, the most important factor is collecting identifiable samples of as many of the different species present as possible. Unfortunately, these methods are not always compatible. The taxonomist sometimes overlooks whole species in favour of those groups currently under study, while the ecologist often collects only a limited number of specimens of each species, thus reducing their value for taxonomic investigations.

To collect as wide a range of species as possible, several methods must be used. These include hand collecting, using baits to attract the ants, ground litter sampling, and the use of pitfall traps. Hand collecting consists of searching for ants everywhere they are likely to occur. This includes on the ground, under rocks, logs or other objects on the ground, in rotten wood on the ground or on trees, in vegetation, on tree trunks and under bark. When possible, collections should be made from nests or foraging columns and at least 20 to 25 individuals collected. This will ensure that all individuals are of the same species, and so increase their value for detailed studies. Since some species are largely nocturnal, collecting should not be confined to daytime. Specimens are collected using an aspirator (often called a pooter), forceps, a fine, moistened paint brush, or fingers, if the ants are known not to sting. Individual insects are placed in plastic or glass tubes (1.5–3.0 ml capacity for small ants, 5–8 ml for larger ants) containing 75% to 95% ethanol. Plastic tubes with secure tops are better than glass because they are lighter, and do not break as easily if mishandled.

Baits can be used to attract and concentrate foragers. This often increases the number of individuals collected and attracts species that are otherwise elusive. Sugars and meats or oils will attract different species and a range should be utilised. These baits can be placed either on the ground or on the trunks of trees or large shrubs. When placed on the ground, baits should be situated on small paper cards or other flat, light-coloured surfaces, or in test-tubes or vials. This makes it easier to spot ants and to capture them before they can escape into the surrounding leaf litter.

Many ants are small and forage primarily in the layer of leaves and other debris on the ground. Collecting these species by hand can be difficult. One of the most successful ways to collect them is to gather the leaf litter in which they are foraging and extract the ants from it. This is most commonly done by placing leaf litter on a screen over a large funnel, often under some heat. As the leaf litter dries from above, ants (and other animals) move downward and eventually fall out the bottom and are collected in alcohol placed below the funnel. This method works especially well in rain forests and marshy areas. A method of improving the catch when using a funnel is to sift the leaf litter through a coarse screen before placing it above the funnel. This will concentrate the litter and remove larger leaves and twigs. It will also allow more litter to be sampled when using a limited number of funnels.

The pitfall trap is another commonly used tool for collecting ants. A pitfall trap can be any small container placed in the ground with the top level with the surrounding surface and filled with a preservative. Ants are collected when they fall into the trap while foraging. The diameter of the traps can vary from about 18 mm to 10 cm and the number used can vary from a few to several hundred. The size of the traps used is influenced largely by personal preference (although larger sizes are generally better), while the number will be determined by the study being undertaken. The preservative used is usually ethylene glycol or propylene glycol, as alcohol will evaporate quickly and the traps will dry out. One advantage of pitfall traps is that they can be used to collect over a period of time with minimal maintenance and intervention. One disadvantage is that some species are not collected as they either avoid the traps or do not commonly encounter them while foraging.

Questions 27–30

Do the following statements agree with the information given in Reading Passage 3?

In boxes 27–30 on your answer sheet, write

> **TRUE**   *if the statement agrees with the information*
> **FALSE**   *if the statement contradicts the information*
> **NOT GIVEN**   *if there is no information on this*

27   Taxonomic research involves comparing members of one group of ants.

28   New species of ant are frequently identified by taxonomists.

29   Range is the key criterion for ecological collections.

30   A single collection of ants can generally be used for both taxonomic and ecological purposes.

Questions 31–36

Classify the following statements as referring to

> **A**   hand collecting
> **B**   using bait
> **C**   sampling ground litter
> **D**   using a pitfall trap

*Write the correct letter, **A**, **B**, **C** or **D**, in boxes 31–36 on your answer sheet.*

31   It is preferable to take specimens from groups of ants.

32   It is particularly effective for wet habitats.

33   It is a good method for species which are hard to find.

34   Little time and effort is required.

35   Separate containers are used for individual specimens.

36   Non-alcoholic preservative should be used.

Questions 37–40

Label the diagram below.

*Choose **NO MORE THAN TWO WORDS** from the passage for each answer.*

Write your answers in boxes 37–40 on your answer sheet.

One method of collecting ants

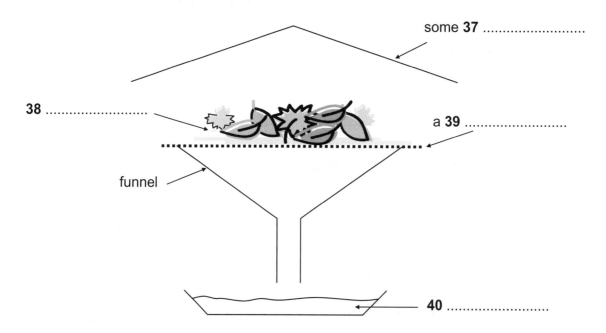

some **37** ....

38 ....

a **39** ....

funnel

40 ....

WRITING TASK 1

You should spend about 20 minutes on this task.

> *The graph below shows the quantities of goods transported in the UK between 1974 and 2002 by four different modes of transport.*
>
> *Summarise the information by selecting and reporting the main features, and make comparisons where relevant.*

Write at least 150 words.

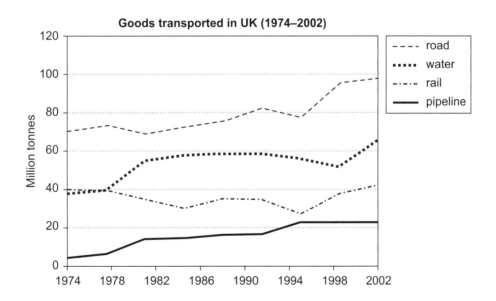

WRITING TASK 2

You should spend about 40 minutes on this task.

Write about the following topic:

In some countries the average weight of people is increasing and their levels of health and fitness are decreasing.

What do you think are the causes of these problems and what measures could be taken to solve them?

Give reasons for your answer and include any relevant examples from your own knowledge or experience.

Write at least 250 words.

SPEAKING

PART 1

The examiner asks the candidate about him/herself, his/her home, work or studies and other familiar topics.

EXAMPLE

Television

- How often do you watch television? [Why/Why not?]
- Which television channel do you usually watch? [Why?]
- Do you enjoy the advertisements on television? [Why/Why not?]
- Do you think most programmes on television are good? [Why/Why not?]

PART 2

> **Describe a friend of your family you remember from your childhood.**
>
> **You should say:**
>   **who the person was**
>   **how your family knew this person**
>   **how often this person visited your family**
> **and explain why you remember this person.**

You will have to talk about the topic for one to two minutes. You have one minute to think about what you are going to say. You can make some notes to help you if you wish.

PART 3

Discussion topics:

Friendship

Example questions:
What do you think makes someone a good friend to a whole family?
Do you think we meet different kinds of friend at different stages of our lives? In what ways are these types of friend different?
How easy is it to make friends with people from a different age group?

Influence of friends

Example questions:
Do you think it is possible to be friends with someone if you never meet them in person? Is this real friendship?
What kind of influence can friends have on our lives?
How important would you say it is to have friends from different cultures?

General Training Reading and Writing Test A

SECTION 1 Questions 1–14

Read the text below and answer Questions 1–6.

	HOLIDAY PLUS					
	*Need a break? Choose from these three wonderful holidays!*					
	Holiday location	**Price***	**Number of nights**	**Daily meals included in package**	**Comments**	**Transport to/ from airport**
A	*Mountain Lodge* a unique wilderness retreat on the edge of the World Heritage-listed National Park and only 5 km from the sea	$330	1	mountain buffet breakfast *plus* free soft drinks always available	free canoeing free talks in the evening free open-air tennis courts horse-riding optional extra	self-drive auto 1 hour 15 minutes *or* bus three times/week approx. 2 hours
B	*Pelican Resort* a true coral island right on the Great Barrier Reef swim straight from the beach	$580	4	hot breakfast *plus* beach picnic lunch *plus* set 4-course dinner	refurbishment: resort will close for May free minibus trip around island plane flights to Wilson Island only $50	½ hour by minibus
C	*Cedar Lodge* a blend of casual sophistication and rich rainforest ambience for those over 25	$740	4	tropical breakfast picnic lunch – optional extra	oldest living rainforest free bikes and tennis courts; horse-riding extra	10 mins by taxi

* Price: per person, per package, twin share

Questions 1–3

*Look at the three holidays, **A**, **B** and **C**, on page 104.*

For which holiday are the following statements true?

*Write the correct letter, **A**, **B** or **C**, in boxes 1–3 on your answer sheet.*

1   This holiday doesn't cater for young children.

2   This holiday provides a tour at no extra cost.

3   This holiday involves most travel time from the airport.

Questions 4–6

Answer the questions below.

*Choose **NO MORE THAN THREE WORDS** from the text for each answer.*

Write your answers in boxes 4–6 on your answer sheet.

4   When will one of the holiday locations not be open?

5   Which two outdoor activities are provided at no extra cost at Mountain Lodge?

6   What is the fastest way to travel to Mountain Lodge?

Read the text below and answer Questions 7–14.

SYDNEY TRAVEL COLLEGE

At this College we recommend the Multiplan policy.

Travel insurance requirements

As this course includes a total of three months' travel outside Australia, travel insurance is compulsory. If you are sick or have an accident in Australia, your medical bills will be fully covered – however, you cannot assume that *everything* will be covered overseas, so please read the following requirements carefully.

1   Medical

Australia has reciprocal medical arrangements with the governments of the eight nations you will be visiting. This arrangement will cover all emergency hospital treatment. However, students will have to take out insurance such as Multiplan to cover the costs of all visits to doctors, and other non-emergency medical situations.

If you have a serious accident or illness, Multiplan insurance will cover the cost of your flight back to Australia, if required. Depending on the circumstances, this may also pay for either medical personnel or a family member to accompany you home. Multiplan insurance may not cover all pre-existing medical conditions – so before you leave be sure to check with them about any long-term illnesses or disabilities that you have.

If you do require medical treatment overseas, and you want to make a claim on your insurance, the claim will not be accepted unless you produce both your student card and your travel insurance card.

2   Belongings

The Multiplan policy covers most student requirements. In particular, it provides students with luggage insurance. This covers any loss or theft of your everyday belongings.
For example, this insurance covers:
• the present value of items that are stolen – provided that you have purchase receipts for every item; if no receipts, no payment can be made
• replacement value of your briefcase or backpack and study books
• portable computers and CD players, if you specifically list them as items in the policy

3   Cancellation

This insurance covers any non-refundable deposit and other costs you have paid if you have to cancel due to 'unforeseen or unforeseeable circumstances outside your control'. It does not provide cover if you change your study or travel plans for other reasons.

Questions 7–14

Classify the following events as being

      A   *covered by government arrangements*
      B   *covered by the Multiplan policy*
      C   *not covered by the Multiplan policy*
      D   *covered in some situations*

*Write the correct letter, **A**, **B**, **C** or **D**, in boxes 7–14 on your answer sheet.*

7   A student travelling overseas suddenly needs hospital treatment.

8   A student consults a doctor regarding a minor problem while abroad.

9   A parent goes overseas to bring an injured or sick student to Australia.

10 A student is treated overseas for an illness he/she had before leaving Australia.

11 A student who requires medical treatment has lost his/her travel insurance card.

12 A student's study books are lost.

13 A student's laptop is stolen.

14 A student changes his/her mind about plans to study and decides not to take the booked flight.

SECTION 2   *Questions 15–27*

Read the text below and answer Questions 15–20.

Kenichi Software: security guidelines for staff

General

It is in everyone's interest to maintain a high level of security in the workplace. You should immediately challenge any person who appears to be on the premises without proper authorisation, or inform a senior member of staff about any odd or unusual activity.

Company Property

You are advised that it is within the company's legal rights to detain any person on the grounds that they may be involved in the unauthorised removal of company property. The company reserves the right to search staff members leaving or entering the premises and to inspect any article or motor vehicle on company property. It is a condition of employment that you submit to such action if requested.

It is in your own interest to ensure that you have proper authority before removing any item of company property from a company building. Any member found removing company property from the building without proper authority will be subject to disciplinary action.

Identity Badges

You will be issued with an identity badge, which should be worn at all times when you are on company premises. The purpose of these badges is to safeguard our security. Badges are issued by Human Resources, and contractors and people visiting the company on a one-off basis are also obliged to wear them.

Confidential Matters

In the course of your work you may have access to information relating to the company's business, or that of a supplier or customer. Such material, even where it appears comparatively trivial, can have a serious effect on the company, supplier or customer if it falls into the wrong hands. It is, therefore, essential that you should at all times be aware of the serious view the company would take of disclosure of such material to outsiders.

You must treat as confidential all information, data, specifications, drawings and all documents relating to the company's business and/or its trading activities, and not divulge, use, or employ them except in the company's service. Before you leave the company, you must hand over to your manager all private notes relevant to the company's business, activities, prices, accounts, costs etc. Legal proceedings may be initiated for any misuse or unauthorised disclosure of such confidential information, whether during employment or afterwards.

Questions 15–20

Complete the sentences below.

*Choose **NO MORE THAN TWO WORDS** from the text for each answer.*

Write your answers in boxes 15–20 on your answer sheet.

15 If you see anything suspicious, you should report it to a .... employee.

16 If the company wants to stop you and .... you, you have to agree to it.

17 If you take things belonging to the company without permission, you will face ....

18 Staff, ... and visitors must all wear a badge on company premises.

19 You must not pass on confidential information to ....

20 If you leave the company, you have to hand in any .... you have made on matters concerning the company.

Read the text below and answer Questions 21–27.

Is Everyone Entitled To Paid Holidays?

The Working Time Regulations (WTRs) introduced a new right to paid holidays for most workers. However, some workers were not covered when the WTRs came into force in October 1998. Since the regulations were amended, with effect from 1 August 2003, the majority of these workers have been entitled to paid holidays, and since 1 August 2004 the regulations have also applied to junior doctors.

Workers who qualify are entitled to no fewer than four weeks of paid holiday a year, and public holidays (normally eight days in England and Wales) count towards this. However, workers and employers can agree longer holidays.

For the first year of work, special accrual rules apply. For each month of employment, workers are entitled to one twelfth of the annual holiday. After the first year of employment, you can take your holiday entitlement at any time, with your employer's approval.

Before taking holidays, you must give your employer notice of at least twice the length of the holiday you want to take: for instance, to take a five-day holiday, you must give at least ten days' notice. If your employer does not want you to take that holiday, they can give you counter-notice equal to the holiday – for example, five days' notice not to take a five-day holiday.

If the employer wants you to take holiday at a given time, e.g. when there is a shutdown at the same time every year, they must give you notice of at least twice the length of the holiday. There is no right for the worker to take that holiday at a different time.

Holiday cannot be carried over to the next year, unless your contract of employment allows this to happen. Nor can you be paid in lieu of your holiday. However, when you leave the job, you are entitled to receive payment for any outstanding holiday, provided your contract specifically allows for this.

It may be that your contract gives you better rights, or your holiday rights might be specified in a collective agreement. Your union representative can advise you on this.

Questions 21–27

Answer the questions below.

*Choose **NO MORE THAN THREE WORDS AND/OR A NUMBER** from the text for each answer.*

Write your answers in boxes 21–27 on your answer sheet.

21 In what year were the regulations extended to cover most of the workers who were originally excluded?

22 What is the minimum annual paid holiday which workers are entitled to?

23 During a worker's first year of employment, what proportion of their annual holiday does a month's work give?

24 What can an employer give a worker to stop them taking holiday that they have requested?

25 What is given as a possible reason for an employee having to take a holiday at a certain time?

26 When an employee leaves their job, what should be given in place of any holiday they have not taken?

27 Apart from a contract, what type of document may set out an employee's holiday rights?

SECTION 3   *Questions 28–40*

Questions 28–33

*The text on pages 113 and 114 has eight sections, **A–H**.*

*Choose the correct heading for sections **C–H** from the list of headings below.*

*Write the correct number, **i–xi**, in boxes 28–33 on your answer sheet.*

List of Headings

i	Where to buy the best Echinacea
ii	What 'snake oil' contained
iii	Growing Echinacea
iv	How to use the Echinacea plant
v	Earlier applications of Echinacea
vi	The origins of the term 'snake oil'
vii	Early research into the effectiveness of Echinacea
viii	How 'snake oil' was first invented
ix	The use of Echinacea in new locations
x	Modern evidence of the effectiveness of Echinacea
xi	Early kinds of 'snake oil'

Examples	*Answers*
Section **A**	**vi**
Section **B**	**xi**

---

28   Section **C**

29   Section **D**

30   Section **E**

31   Section **F**

32   Section **G**

33   Section **H**

Snake Oil

A Back in the days of America's Wild West, when cowboys roamed the range and people were getting themselves caught up in gunfights, a new phrase – 'snake oil' – entered the language. It was a dismissive term for the patent medicines, often useless, sold by travelling traders who always claimed miraculous cures for everything from baldness to snakebite.

Selling 'snake oil' was almost as risky a business as cattle stealing; you might be run out of town if your particular medicine, as you realised it would, failed to live up to its claims. Consequently, the smarter 'snake oil' sellers left town before their customers had much chance to evaluate the 'cure' they had just bought.

B The remarkable thing about many of the medicines dismissed then as 'snake oil' is not so much that they failed to live up to the outrageous claims made for them – those that weren't harmless coloured water could be positively dangerous. What's remarkable is that so many of the claims made for some of these remedies, or at least their ingredients, most of them plant based, have since been found to have at least some basis in fact.

One, Echinacea, eventually turned out to be far more potent than even its original promoter claimed. Echinacea first appeared in 'Meyer's Blood Purifier', promoted as a cure-all by a Dr H.C.F. Meyer – a lay doctor with no medical qualifications. 'Meyer's Blood Purifier' claimed not only to cure snakebite, but also to eliminate a host of other ailments.

C Native to North America, the roots of Echinacea, or purple coneflower, had been used by the Plains Indians for all kinds of ailments long before Meyer came along. They applied poultices of it to wounds and stings, used it for teeth and gum disease and made a tea from it to treat everything from colds and measles to arthritis. They even used it for snakebite.

D Settlers quickly picked up on the plant's usefulness but until Meyer sent samples of his 'blood purifier' to John Lloyd, a pharmacist, it remained a folk remedy. Initially dismissing Meyer's claims as nonsense, Lloyd was eventually converted after a colleague, John King, tested the herb and successfully used it to treat bee stings and nasal congestion.

In fact, he went much further in his claims than Meyer ever did and by the 1890s a bottle of tincture[1] of Echinacea could be found in almost every American home, incidentally making a fortune for Lloyd's company, Lloyd Brothers Pharmacy.

E As modern antibiotics became available, the use of Echinacea products declined and from the 1940s to the 1970s it was pretty much forgotten in the USA. It was a different story in Europe, where both French and German herbalists and homeopaths continued to make extensive use of it.

---

[1] a liquid containing a special ingredient

It had been introduced there by Gerhard Madaus, who travelled from Germany to America in 1937, returning with seed to establish commercial plots of Echinacea. His firm conducted extensive research on echinacin, a concentrate they made from the juice of flowering tops of the plants he had brought back. It was put into ointments, liquids for internal and external use, and into products for injections.

F   There is no evidence that Echinacea is effective against snakebite, but Dr Meyer – who genuinely believed in Echinacea – would probably be quite amused if he could come back and see the uses to which modern science has put 'his' herb. He might not be surprised that science has confirmed Echinacea's role as a treatment for wounds, or that it has been found to be helpful in relieving arthritis, both claims Meyer made for the herb.

He might though be surprised to learn how Echinacea is proving to be an effective weapon against all sorts of disease, particularly infections. German researchers had used it successfully to treat a range of infections and found it to be effective against bacteria and protozoa[2].

There are many other intriguing medical possibilities for extracts from the herb, but its apparent ability to help with our more common ailments has seen thousands of people become enthusiastic converts. Dozens of packaged products containing extracts of Echinacea can now be found amongst the many herbal remedies and supplements on the shelves of health stores and pharmacies. Many of those might be the modern equivalents of 'snake oil', but Echinacea at least does seem to have some practical value.

G   Echinacea is a dry prairie plant, drought-resistant and pretty tolerant of most soils, although it does best in good soil with plenty of sun. Plants are usually grown from seed but they are sometimes available from nurseries. Echinacea is a distinctive perennial with erect, hairy, spotted stems up to a metre tall. Flower heads look like daisies, with purple rayed florets and a dark brown central cone. The leaves are hairy; the lower leaves are oval to lance-shaped and coarsely and irregularly toothed.

H   There are nine species of Echinacea in all but only three are generally grown for medicinal use. All have similar medicinal properties. Most European studies have used liquid concentrates extracted from the tops of plants, whereas extraction in the USA has usually been from the roots. Today most manufacturers blend both, sometimes adding flowers and seeds to improve the quality.

For the home grower, the roots of all species seem equally effective. Dig them up in autumn after the tops have died back after the first frost. Wash and dry them carefully and store them in glass containers. You can harvest the tops throughout the summer and even eat small amounts of leaf straight from the plant.

Even if you don't make your fortune from this herb, there are few sights more attractive than a field of purple coneflowers in all their glory. And with a few Echinacea plants nearby, you'll never go short of a cure.

---

[2]   a type of micro-organism

Questions 34–40

Do the following statements agree with the information given in the text?

In boxes 34–40 on your answer sheet, write

TRUE	*if the statement agrees with the information*
FALSE	*if the statement contradicts the information*
NOT GIVEN	*if there is no information on this*

34 'Snake oil' sellers believed their product was effective.

35 Most people in the Wild West mistrusted 'snake oil'.

36 Some 'snake oils' were mostly water.

37 All 'snake oils' contained Echinacea.

38 Echinacea has been proven to kill microbes.

39 The highest quality Echinacea is grown in America.

40 More than one part of the Echinacea plant has a medicinal use.

WRITING

WRITING TASK 1

You should spend about 20 minutes on this task.

You have recently moved to a different house.

Write a letter to an English-speaking friend. In your letter

- *explain why you have moved*
- *describe the new house*
- *invite your friend to come and visit*

Write at least 150 words.

You do NOT need to write any addresses.

Begin your letter as follows:

Dear .... ,

WRITING TASK 2

You should spend about 40 minutes on this task.

Write about the following topic:

Today more people are travelling than ever before.

Why is this the case?

What are the benefits of travelling for the traveller?

Give reasons for your answer and include any relevant examples from your own knowledge or experience.

Write at least 250 words.

General Training Reading and Writing Test B

SECTION 1   *Questions 1–14*

Read the text below and answer Questions 1–8.

Consumer advice on buying shoes

If you have a problem with shoes you've recently bought, follow this four-step plan.

Step 1

Go back to the shop with proof of purchase. If you return faulty shoes at once, you have a right to insist on a refund. It is also likely that you will get one if you change your mind about the shoes and take them back immediately. But, if you delay or you've had some use out of the shoes, the shop may not give you all your money back. It depends on the state of the shoes and how long you've had them.

If you are offered a credit note, you don't have to accept it. If you accept it, you will usually not be able to exchange it for cash later on. So, you may be left with an unwanted credit note, if you cannot find any other shoes you want from the shop.

The shop may want to send the shoes back to head office for inspection. This is fair and could help to sort things out. But don't be put off by the shop which claims that it's the manufacturer's responsibility. This isn't true. It's the shop's legal duty to put things right.

Step 2

If you don't seem to be getting anywhere, you can get help. Free advice is available from a Citizens Advice Bureau (get the address from your telephone book), or from a local Trading Standards Department. Again, consult the telephone directory under County, Regional or Borough Council. All these departments have people who can advise you about faulty goods and what to do with them.

Step 3

Most shops are covered by the Footwear Code of Practice. If the shop you are dealing with is covered, you can ask for the shoes to be sent to the Footwear Testing Centre for an independent opinion. The shop has to agree with whatever the resulting report says. There is a charge of £21. You pay £7 and the shop pays the rest (including postage).

Step 4

As a last resort, you can take your case to court. This is not as difficult as it sounds. The small claims procedure for amounts up to £1000 (£750 in Scotland) is a cheap, easy and informal way of taking legal action.

The relevant forms are available from your nearest County Court or, in Scotland, the Sheriff Court. You can get advice and leaflets from the Citizens Advice Bureau. Alternatively, some bookshops sell advice packs which contain the relevant forms.

Questions 1–8

Do the following statements agree with the information given in the text on page 117?

In boxes 1–8 on your answer sheet, write

> **TRUE**   *if the statement agrees with the information*
> **FALSE**   *if the statement contradicts the information*
> **NOT GIVEN**   *if there is no information on this*

1   If you return unwanted shoes straightaway, with a receipt, the shop will probably give you a refund.

2   You are advised to accept a credit note if you are offered one.

3   The factory is responsible for replacing unwanted shoes.

4   You can ask any shoe shop to send shoes to the Footwear Testing Centre.

5   Shops prefer to give a credit note rather than change shoes.

6   The customer contributes to the cost of having faulty shoes tested.

7   The procedure for making a legal claim is easier in Scotland.

8   Legal advice and forms can be bought from certain shops.

Read the text below and answer Questions 9–14.

LOST CARDS

If you discover that your credit card, cheque book, debit card or cash card is missing, telephone the credit card company or bank as soon as possible. Follow this up with a letter. If you suspect theft, tell the police as well. In most circumstances, provided you act quickly, you will not have to pay any bills which a thief runs up on your account. Most home insurance policies will also cover you against even this limited risk.

Because plastic money is now so common, central registration schemes such as Credit Card Shield and Card Protection System exist to help customers whose cards are lost or stolen. Under the schemes you file details of all your cards – including cash cards and account cards issued by shops – with a central registry, for a small annual fee. Then, if any or all of your cards are stolen, you need to make only one phone call to the registry, which is open around the clock 365 days a year. As soon as you have called, your responsibility for any bills run up by the thief ends and the scheme's staff make sure that all the companies whose cards you had are notified.

What you stand to lose on a stolen card

CREDIT CARD You will not have to pay more than £50 of the bills a thief runs up with your card. If you report the loss before the card is used, you will not have to pay anything.

CHEQUES AND GUARANTEE CARD Unless you have been careless – by signing blank cheques, say – you will not have to pay for any forged cheques a thief uses. The bank or shop that accepts them will have to bear the loss.

DEBIT CARD (Switch or Visa Delta) The banks operate a system similar to that for credit cards, in that you are liable for bills up to £50.

If your cash card is stolen

Legally, you can be made to pay back any sums a thief withdraws using your card, but only up to the time you report the loss and up to £50, unless the bank can prove gross negligence, such as writing your personal identification number on your card.

- Never keep your card and a note of your personal number (which does not appear on the card) together.
- Memorise your personal number if possible. If you must make a note of it, disguise it as something else – a telephone number, say.
- The same rules and precautions apply to a credit card used as a cash card.

Questions 9–14

*Choose the correct letter, **A**, **B**, **C** or **D**.*

Write the correct letter in boxes 9–14 on your answer sheet.

9 What should you do first if you lose a credit card?

 A   contact your insurance company
 B   write a letter
 C   contact the police
 D   make a phone call

10 Credit Card Shield is

 A   an insurance company which deals with card theft.
 B   a system for registering people's card details.
 C   an emergency telephone answering service.
 D   an agency for finding lost or stolen cards.

11 When contacted, the Card Protection System company will

 A   inform the police about the loss of the card.
 B   get in touch with the relevant credit card companies.
 C   ensure that lost cards are replaced.
 D   give details about the loss of the card to shops.

12 You are fully covered by both banks and shops if you lose

 A   a cheque that is signed but not otherwise completed.
 B   a blank unsigned cheque.
 C   a Switch card.
 D   a credit card.

13 If you have written your personal number on a stolen card, you may have to

 A   join a different credit card protection scheme.
 B   pay up to £50 for any loss incurred.
 C   pay for anything the thief buys on it.
 D   change your account to a different bank.

14 What happens if your cash card is stolen?

 A   You arrange for the card to be returned.
 B   The bank stops you withdrawing money.
 C   You may have to pay up to £50 of any stolen money.
 D   You cannot use a cash card in future.

SECTION 2   *Questions 15–27*

Read the text on pages 121 and 122 and answer Questions 15–21.

Recycling at work – handy hints to employers

It is estimated that avoidable waste costs UK businesses up to 4.5% of their annual revenue. Reducing waste in the workplace is about being efficient. By becoming more efficient, businesses not only increase profits but they also save natural resources.

On the island of Jersey, for example, the amount of waste produced each year has doubled since 1980. In 2004 it topped 100,000 tonnes – and 60% is generated by local businesses. A lot of waste for a small island!

Setting up a company scheme

Waste audit
Before starting a recycling scheme, perform an audit. This will make you aware of how much waste you are producing in the company.

Company policy
Consider switching your office waste contractor to one that provides a recycling service.

Buy recycled paper. Although this is sometimes more expensive, costs can be reduced by lowering consumption and using duplex printers.

Get everyone involved
- Raise awareness internally within the company, perhaps by putting up educational posters.
- Allocate a person to be the point of contact for anyone with queries.

There are also a couple of ways to increase motivation:
- Hold internal competitions between different departments. For example, see which can reduce their waste the most within a specific time period.
- Send out regular newsletters reporting on all waste improvements. Staff will then see the impact their actions are having.

What to recycle and how

Paper

According to a recent survey, 65% of waste produced is paper waste. Waste paper will inevitably be produced in the workplace, but it is not necessary to discard it. It can serve a variety of purposes before it is recycled, such as writing notes. Envelopes too can be re-used for internal mail.

Plastic cups

Rather than supplying disposable plastic cups in your workplace, get ceramic mugs that can be re-used. Not only do they make your tea taste better, but they can reduce your office waste by up to 1%!

Electrical equipment

Rather than giving up on any old electrical equipment and just throwing it away, why not try upgrading it? This reduces waste, as well as avoiding the need to manufacture a new machine – a process which creates a large amount of waste. You could also consider donating your old computers to charities when it comes to replacing them.

Questions 15–21

Answer the questions below.

*Choose **NO MORE THAN TWO WORDS** from the text for each answer.*

Write your answers in boxes 15–21 on your answer sheet.

15 What does the writer think should be carried out in a company before it starts recycling?

16 What machines can help to cut the stationery budget?

17 What can be displayed in the workplace to publicise the recycling scheme?

18 What can be distributed to motivate staff to recycle more?

19 What can unwanted paper be used for in the office?

20 What can be bought to cut down on the waste produced by staff refreshments?

21 Where can unwanted PCs be sent?

Read the text below and answer Questions 22–27.

How to answer any interview question

To start, take a tip from consultants who coach executives on how to handle media interviews. They say you can deliver the message you want to an employer, regardless of the question you're asked.

'Unlike some politicians, who take no notice of press questions and immediately introduce a different topic in response, job candidates must answer employers' queries,' says John Barford of the interview training firm Genesis. 'However, you can quickly make the transition from your answer to the important points you want to convey about your qualifications,' he says.

He advises candidates at job interviews to apply the formula Q = A + 1: Q is the question; A is the answer; + is the bridge to the message you want to deliver; and 1 is the point you want to make.

Diligent preparation is also necessary to effectively answer any interview question, say senior executives. They give a number of useful tips:

- Learn as much as you can beforehand. Ask company employees questions prior to job interviews to gain as much insight as you can. If the company is publicly owned, find out how viable it is by reading shareholder reports. You can then tailor what you say to the company's issues.
- Be prepared for questions that require you to show how you handled difficult challenges. These questions require stories in response, but as it's unlikely that you'll have one that fits every situation, try to recall some from your past experience that show how you coped with a range of issues.
- Count on being asked about a past mistake or blemish on your career record, and don't try to dodge the issue. Ms Murphy, president of the Murphy Group, a media interview training firm, says that it's important to steer clear of lies at all costs. Just answer the question and move on.
- When discussing a mistake, focus on the positive outcomes. 'You learn as much by dropping the ball as you do by catching it,' says senior executive Mr Friedmann. When he was being interviewed for his current job, he mentioned he had been involved in many successful turnarounds and one that failed. 'And I said how I'd benefited in many ways from going through that experience,' he says.

Questions 22–27

Complete the sentences below.

*Choose **NO MORE THAN TWO WORDS** from the text for each answer.*

Write your answers in boxes 22–27 on your answer sheet.

22   The writer warns candidates not to imitate the way that .... ignore questions in interviews.

23   Interviewees are recommended to follow a certain .... to allow them to communicate their main points.

24   Senior executives advise candidates to request information from .... before an interview.

25   A candidate can also learn about a business by studying its ....

26   The head of an interview training firm advises people to avoid telling ....

27   In his job interview, one executive explained how he had .... considerably from a previous failure.

SECTION 3   *Questions 28–40*

Read the text on pages 125 and 126 and answer Questions 28–40.

TALKING POINT

Learning a second language fuels children's intelligence and makes their job prospects brighter. But the fact is, in New Zealand, as in many other English-speaking countries, speakers of two or more languages are in the minority. Eighty-four per cent of New Zealanders are monolingual (speakers of only one language). This leaves a small number who claim to speak two or more languages – a small percentage of whom were born in New Zealand.

No matter how proud people are of their cultural roots, to speak anything other than English is a marker of difference here. That's why eight-year-old Tiffany Dvorak no longer wishes to speak her mother-tongue, German, and eight-year-old Ani Powell is embarrassed when people comment on the fact that she is able to speak Maori*. As Joanne Powell, Ani's mother, points out: 'In Europe, it's not unusual for kids to be bilingual. But, if you speak another language to your children in New Zealand, there are some people who think that you are not helping them to become a member of society.'

But in fact, the general agreement among experts is that learning a second language is good for children. Experts believe that bilinguals – people who speak two languages – have a clear learning advantage over their monolingual schoolmates. This depends on how much of each language they can speak, not on which language is used, so it doesn't matter whether they are learning Maori or German or Chinese or any other language.

Cathie Elder, a professor of Language Teaching and Learning at Auckland University, says: 'A lot of studies have shown that children who speak more than one language sometimes learn one language more slowly, but in the end they do as well as their monolingual schoolmates, and often better, in other subjects. The view is that there is an improvement in general intelligence from the effort of learning another language.'

Dr Brigitte Halford, a professor of linguistics at Freiburg University in Germany, agrees. 'Bilinguals tend to use language better as a whole,' she says. 'They also display greater creativity and problem-solving ability, and they learn further languages more easily.'

So with all of the benefits, why do we not show more enthusiasm for learning other languages? Parents and teachers involved in bilingual education say pressure from friends at school, general attitudes to other languages in English-speaking countries, and problems in the school system are to blame.

In New Zealand, immigrants face the possibility of culture being lost along with the language their children no longer wish to speak. Tiffany's mother, Susanne Dvorak, has experienced this. When she and husband Dieter left Germany six years ago to start up a new life in New Zealand, they thought it would be the perfect opportunity to raise their two-year-old as a bilingual. After all, bilingual Turkish families in Germany were normal and Susanne had read all the books she could find on the subject.

---

*   Maori: the language spoken by the Maori people, the first native people of New Zealand

The idea was to have home as a German language environment and for Tiffany to learn English at nursery school. But when Tiffany went to nursery school she stopped talking completely. She was quiet for about two or three months. Then, when she took up talking again, it was only in English. Concerned for her language development, Dieter started speaking English to his daughter while Susanne continued in German.

Today, when Susanne speaks to her daughter in German, she still answers in English. 'Or sometimes she speaks half and half. I checked with her teacher and she very seldom mixes up German and English at school. She speaks English like a New Zealander. It's her German that's behind,' says Susanne.

Professor Halford, also a mother of two bilingual children, says, 'It's normal for kids to refuse to speak their home language at the stage when they start to socialise with other kids in kindergarten or school'. But, she says, this depends a lot on the attitudes of the societies in question. In monolingual societies, like New Zealand, 'kids want to be like all the others and sometimes use bilingualism as one of the battlefields for finding their own identity in contrast to that of their parents.'

She supports Susanne's approach of not pressuring her daughter. 'Never force the child to use a specific language, just keep using it yourself. The child will accept that. There is often a time when children or teenagers will need to establish their own identity as different from their schoolmates and they may use their other language to do so.'

Cathie Elder thinks immigrant parents should only speak English to their children if they are able to use English well themselves. 'What parents should do is provide rich language experiences for their children in whatever language they speak well. They may feel like outsiders and want to speak the local language, but it is more important for the child's language development to provide a lot of language experience in any language.'

There can be differences between children in attitudes to learning languages. Susanne Dvorak's two-year-old son, Danyon, is already showing signs of speaking German and English equally well. While her 'ideal' scenario hasn't happened with Tiffany, she is aware that her daughter has a certain bilingual ability which, although mainly passive at this stage, may develop later on.

Joanne Powell feels the same way about her daughter, Ani. 'At the moment she may not want to speak Maori but that's okay because she'll pick it up again in her own time. It's more important that she has the ability to understand who she is. By learning another language she can open the door to another culture.'

Donna Chan, 25, a marketing specialist for IBM, arrived here with her parents from Hong Kong when she was four. She also remembers refusing to speak Chinese when she started primary school. But now she appreciates she had the chance to be bilingual. 'It's quite beneficial speaking another language in my job. Last year, my company sent me to a trade fair in Hong Kong because I could speak Chinese. Being bilingual definitely opens doors,' she says.

Questions 28–31

Do the following statements agree with the information given in the text?

In boxes 28–31 on your answer sheet, write

> **TRUE**   *if the statement agrees with the information*
> **FALSE**   *if the statement contradicts the information*
> **NOT GIVEN** *if there is no information on this*

28   Most people who speak a second language in New Zealand were born in another country.

29   Most New Zealanders believe it is good to teach children a second language.

30   Chinese is the most common foreign language in New Zealand.

31   Some languages develop your intelligence more than others.

Questions 32–38

Look at the following statements (Questions 32–38) and the list of people below.

*Match each statement with the correct person, **A–E**.*

*Write the correct letter, **A–E**, in boxes 32–38 on your answer sheet.*

NB   *You may use any letter more than once.*

32   Children learning two languages may learn one language faster.

33   It has been unexpectedly difficult to raise a bilingual child in New Zealand.

34   Her daughter sometimes speaks a mixture of two languages.

35   Children's attitudes to language depend on general social attitudes.

36   It is not important which language parents speak with their children.

37   Learning a second language provides opportunities to learn another culture.

38   Speaking a second language provides work opportunities.

List of People
A   Cathie Elder
B   Brigitte Halford
C   Susanne Dvorak
D   Joanne Powell
E   Donna Chan

Question 39

*Choose **TWO** letters, **A–F**.*

Write the correct letters in box 39 on your answer sheet.

39 Which **TWO** people stopped speaking one language as a child?

    A   Donna Chan
    B   Susanne Dvorak
    C   Tiffany Dvorak
    D   Cathie Elder
    E   Brigitte Halford
    F   Joanne Powell

Question 40

*Choose **TWO** letters, **A–F**.*

Write the correct letters in box 40 on your answer sheet.

40 Which **TWO** people think that their children's language may develop as they get older?

    A   Donna Chan
    B   Susanne Dvorak
    C   Tiffany Dvorak
    D   Cathie Elder
    E   Brigitte Halford
    F   Joanne Powell

WRITING

WRITING TASK 1

You should spend about 20 minutes on this task.

You recently bought a piece of equipment for your kitchen but it did not work. You phoned the shop but no action was taken.

Write a letter to the shop manager. In your letter

- *describe the problem with the equipment*
- *explain what happened when you phoned the shop*
- *say what you would like the manager to do.*

Write at least 150 words.

You do **NOT** need to write any addresses.

Begin your letter as follows:

Dear Sir or Madam,

WRITING TASK 2

You should spend about 40 minutes on this task.

Write about the following topic:

Some people think that it is better to educate boys and girls in separate schools. Others, however, believe that boys and girls benefit more from attending mixed schools.

Discuss both these views and give your own opinion.

Give reasons for your answer and include any relevant examples from your own knowledge or experience.

Write at least 250 words.

Tapescripts

TEST 1

PART 1

NINA:	Hi, George! Glad you're back. *Loads* of people have phoned you.
GEORGE:	Really?
NINA:	I felt just like your secretary!
GEORGE:	Sorry! I went into the library this afternoon to have a look at a newspaper and I came across something really interesting.
NINA:	What? A book?
GEORGE:	No, a brochure from a summer festival – mainly Spanish music. Look, I've got it here.
NINA:	Spanish music? I really love the guitar. Let's have a look. So what's this group 'Guitarrini'?
GEORGE:	They're really good. They had <u>a video</u> with all the highlights of the festival at a stand in the lobby to the library, so I heard them. They play fantastic instruments – drums and flutes and old kinds of guitars. I've never heard anything like it before.
NINA:	Sounds great.
GEORGE:	Okay. Shall we go then? Spoil ourselves?
NINA:	Yes, let's.
GEORGE:	The only problem is there aren't any cheap seats . . . it's all one price.
NINA:	Well, in that case we could sit right at the front – we'd have a really good view.
GEORGE:	Yeah, though I think that if you sit at the back <u>you can actually hear the whole thing better</u>.
NINA:	Yes. Anyway we can decide when we get there.

Q1

Q2

- -

NINA:	So will you fill in the form or shall I?
GEORGE:	I'll do it. Name: George O'Neill. Address: <u>48 North Avenue</u>, Westsea. Do you remember our new postcode? Still can't remember it.
NINA:	Just a minute – I've got it written down here. <u>WS6 2YH</u>. Do you need the phone too?
GEORGE:	Please. I'm really bad at numbers.
NINA:	<u>01674 553242</u>. So, let's book two tickets for Guitarrini.
GEORGE:	Okay. If you're sure £7.50 each is all right. How do you feel about the singer?
NINA:	I haven't quite decided. But I've noticed something on the booking form that might just persuade me!
GEORGE:	What's that then?
NINA:	Free refreshments!
GEORGE:	Really?

Q3

Q4

Q5

NINA:	Yes, look here. Sunday 17th of June. Singer, ticket £6.00 includes <u>drinks</u> in the garden.	Q6
GEORGE:	Sounds like a bargain to me!	
NINA:	Yes, let's book two tickets for that. So, what else? I'm feeling quite keen now! How about the <u>pianist</u> on the 22nd of June?	Q7
GEORGE:	Anna Ventura? I've just remembered that's my evening class night.	
NINA:	That's okay. I'll just have to go on my own – but we can go to the Spanish dance and guitar concert together, can't we?	
GEORGE:	Yes – I'm sure Tom and Kieran would enjoy that too. Good heavens – <u>£10.50</u> a ticket! I can see we're going to have to go without food for the rest of the week – we'll need to book <u>four</u>!	Q8 Q9
NINA:	Wish we were students – look! Children, Students and Senior Citizens get a <u>50%</u> discount on everything.	Q10
GEORGE:	If only!	

PART 2

Hello, and thank you for asking me to your teachers' meeting to talk about the Dinosaur Museum and to tell you a bit about what you can do with your students there.

Well, let me give you some of the basic information first. In regard to opening hours, we're open every day of the week from 9.00 am to 8.00 pm except on Mondays when we close at <u>1.30 pm</u>. And, in fact the only day in the year when we're closed is on the <u>25th of December</u>. You can book a guided tour for your school group any time that we're open.   Q11 & 12

If you bring a school group to the museum, when you arrive we ask you to remain with your group <u>in the car park. One or more of the tour guides will welcome you there</u> and brief you   Q13
about what the tour will be about. We do this there because our entrance is quite small and we really haven't got much room for briefing groups in the exhibition area.

As far as the amount of time you'll need goes, if you bring a school group you should plan on allowing a minimum of 90 minutes for the visit. This allows 15 minutes to get on and off the coach, <u>45 minutes</u> for the guided tour and 30 minutes for after-tour activities.   Q14

If you're going to have lunch at the museum you will, of course, have to allow more time. There are two cafés in the museum, with seating for 80 people. If you want to eat there you'll need to reserve some seating, as they can get quite crowded at lunch time. Then outside the museum at the back there are <u>tables</u>, and students can bring their own lunch   Q15
and eat it there in the open air.

When the students come into the museum foyer we ask them to check in their backpacks with their books, lunch boxes, etc, at the cloakroom before they enter the museum proper. I'm afraid in the past we have had a few things gone missing after school visits so this is a strict rule. Also, some of the exhibits are fragile and we don't want them to be accidentally knocked. But <u>we do provide school students with handouts with questions and quizzes on</u>   Q16–18
<u>them</u>. There's so much that students can learn in the museum and it's fun for them to have something to do. Of course <u>they'll need to bring something to write with for these. We do</u>   Q16–18
<u>allow students to take photographs</u>. For students who are doing projects it's useful to make some kind of visual record of what they see that they can add to their reports. And finally, they should not bring anything to eat into the museum, or drinks of any kind.

There are also a few things the students can do after the tour. In the theatrette on the ground floor there are continuous <u>screenings of short documentaries about dinosaurs</u>   *Q19 & 20*
<u>which they can see</u> at any time. We used to have an activity room with more interactive things like making models of dinosaurs and drawing and painting pictures, even hunting for dinosaur eggs, but unfortunately the room was damaged in a bad storm recently when water came in the roof, so that's closed at the moment. But we do have an IT centre where students have access to CD ROMs <u>with a range of dinosaur games</u>. These games are a lot *Q19 & 20* of fun, but they also teach the students about the lives of dinosaurs, how they found food, protected their habitat, survived threats, that kind of thing.

And . . . I think that's all I have to tell you. Please feel free to ask any questions if you would like to know anything else . . .

PART 3

TUTOR:	Right, Sandra. You wanted to see me to get some feedback on your group's proposal. The one you're submitting for the Geography Society field trip competition. I've had a look through your proposal and I think it's a really good choice. In fact, I only have a few things to say about it, but even in an outline document like this you really have to be careful to avoid typos and problems with layout in the proposal, and even in the contents page. So read it through carefully before submitting it, okay?
SANDRA:	Will do.
TUTOR:	And I've made a few notes on the proposal about things which <u>could have</u> *Q21* <u>been better sequenced.</u>
SANDRA:	Okay.
TUTOR:	As for the writing itself, I've annotated the proposal as and where I thought it could be improved. Generally speaking, I feel you've often used complex structures and long sentences for the sake of it and as a consequence . . . although your paragraphing and inclusion of sub-headings help . . . it's quite hard to follow your train of thought at times. <u>So</u> *Q22* <u>cut them down a bit, can you?</u>
SANDRA:	Really?
TUTOR:	Yes. And don't forget simple formatting like numbering.
SANDRA:	Didn't I use page numbers?
TUTOR:	I didn't mean that. Look, you've remembered to include headers and footers, which is good, but <u>listing ideas clearly is important</u>. Number them *Q23* or use bullet points, which is even clearer. Then you'll focus the reader on your main points. I thought your suggestion to go to the Navajo Tribal Park was a very good idea.
SANDRA:	I've always wanted to go there. <u>My father was a great fan of cowboy films</u> *Q24* <u>and the Wild West so I was subjected to seeing all the epics, many of</u> <u>which were shot there. As a consequence</u>, it feels very familiar to me and it's awesome both geographically and visually, so <u>it's somewhere I've</u> <u>always wanted to visit.</u> The subsequent research I did and the online photographs made me even keener.

TUTOR:	Interesting. Right, let's look at the content of your proposal now.
SANDRA:	Did you find it comprehensive enough?

TUTOR:	Well, yes and no. You've listed several different topics on your contents page, but I'm not sure they're all relevant.	
SANDRA:	No? Well, I thought that from the perspective of a field trip, one thing I needed <u>to focus on was the sandstone plateaux and cliffs themselves</u>. The way they tower up from the flat landscape is just amazing. The fact that the surrounding softer rocks were eroded by wind and rain, leaving these huge outcrops high above the plain. It's hardly surprising that tourists flock to see the area.	*Q25–27*
TUTOR:	Well, yes, I'd agree with including those points . . .	
SANDRA:	And then the fact that it's been home to native American Navajos and all the social history that goes with that. The hardships they endured trying to save their territory from the invading settlers. Their culture is so rich – all those wonderful stories.	
TUTOR:	Well, I agree it's interesting, but it's not immediately relevant to your proposal, Sandra, so at this stage, I suggest you focus on other considerations. <u>I think an indication of what the students on the trip could actually do when they get there should be far more central</u>, so that certainly needs to be included and to be expanded upon. <u>And I'd like to see something about the local wildlife, and vegetation too</u>, not that I imagine there's much to see. Presumably the tourist invasion hasn't helped.	*Q25–27* *Q25–27*
SANDRA:	Okay, I'll do some work on those two areas as well. But you're right, there's not much apart from some very shallow-rooted species. Although it's cold and snowy there in the winter, the earth is baked so hard in the summer sun that rainwater can't penetrate. So it's a case of flood or drought, really.	
TUTOR:	So, I understand. Now, before we look at everything in more detail, I've got a few factual questions for you. It would be a good idea to include the answers in your finished proposal, because they're missing from your draft.	
SANDRA:	Fine.	
TUTOR:	So, you mentioned the monoliths and the spires, which was good, but what area does the tribal park cover? Do you know?	
SANDRA:	<u>12,000</u> hectares, and the plain is at about 5,850 metres above sea level.	*Q28*
TUTOR:	Larger than I expected. Okay. Where's the nearest accommodation? That's a practical detail that you haven't included. Have you done any research on that?	
SANDRA:	Yes. There's nowhere to stay in the park itself, but there's an old trading post called Goulding quite near. All kinds of tours start from Goulding, too.	
TUTOR:	What kind of tours?	
SANDRA:	Well, the most popular are in four-wheel drive jeeps – but I wouldn't recommend hiring those. I think the best way to appreciate the area would be to hire <u>horses</u> instead and trek around on those. Biking is not allowed and it's impossible to drive around the area in private vehicles. The tracks are too rough.	*Q29*
TUTOR:	Okay, lastly, what else is worth visiting there?	
SANDRA:	There are several <u>caves</u>, but I haven't looked into any details. I'll find out about them.	*Q30*
TUTOR:	Okay, good. Now what I'd like to know is . . .	

PART 4

So, welcome to your introductory geography lecture. We'll begin with some basics. Firstly, what do we learn by studying geography?

Well, we learn a great deal about all the processes that have affected and that continue to affect the earth's <u>surface</u>. But we learn far more than that, because studying geography   *Q31* also informs us about the different kinds of relationships that develop between a particular <u>environment</u> and the people that live there.   *Q32*

Okay. We like to think of geography as having two main branches. There's the study of the nature of our planet – its physical features, what it actually looks like – and then there's the study of the ways in which we choose to live and of the <u>impact</u> of those on our planet. Our   *Q33* current use of carbon fuels is a good example of that.

But there are more specific study areas to consider too, and we'll be looking at each of these in turn throughout this semester. These include bio-physical geography, by which I mean the study of the natural environment and all its living things. Then there's topography – that looks at the shapes of the land and oceans. There's the study of political geography and social geography too, of course, which is the study of communities of people. We have economic geography – in which we examine all kinds of resources and their use – agriculture, for example. Next comes historical geography – the understanding of how people and their environments and the ways they interact have changed over a period of time – and <u>urban</u> geography, an aspect I'm particularly interested in, which takes as its   *Q34* focus the location of cities, the services that those cities provide, and migration of people to and from such cities. And lastly, we have cartography. That's the art and science of map-making. You'll be doing a lot of that!

So, to summarise before we continue, we now have our key answer . . . studying this subject is important because without geographical knowledge, we would know very little about our surroundings and we wouldn't be able to identify all the <u>problems</u> that relate to   *Q35* them. So, by definition, we wouldn't be in an informed position to work out how to solve any of them.

Okay, now for some practicalities. What do geographers actually do? Well, we collect data to begin with! You'll be doing a lot of that on your first field trip! How do we do this? There are several means. We might, for example, conduct a census – count a population in a given area perhaps. We also need <u>images</u> of the earth's surface which we can produce by   *Q36* means of computer-generation technology or with the help of satellite relays. We've come a very long way from the early exploration of the world by sailing ships when geographers only had pens and paper at their disposal.

After we've gathered our information, we must analyse it! We need to look for <u>patterns</u>,   *Q37* most commonly those of causes and consequences. This kind of information helps us to predict and resolve problems that could affect the world we live in.

But we don't keep all this information confidential. We then need to publish our findings so that other people can access it and be informed by it. And one way in which this information can be published is in the form of maps. You'll all have used one at some stage of your life already. Let's consider the benefits of maps from a geographer's perspective.

Maps can be folded and put in a pocket and can provide a great store of reference when they're collected into an atlas. They can depict the physical features of the entire planet if necessary, or, just a small part of it in much greater detail. But there is a drawback. You can't exactly replicate something that is three-dimensional, like our planet, on a flat piece of paper, because paper has only two dimensions, and that means there'll always be a certain degree of <u>distortion</u> on a map. It can't be avoided.   *Q38*

We can also use aerial photographs . . . pictures taken by cameras at high altitude above the earth. These are great for showing all kinds of geographical features that are not easy to see from the ground. You can easily illustrate areas of diseased trees or how much <u>traffic</u> is on the roads at a given time or information about deep sea beds, for example.   *Q39*

Then there are Landsats. These are satellites that circle the earth and transmit visual information to computers at receiving stations. They circle the earth several times a day and can provide a mass of information – you'll all be familiar with the information they give us about the <u>weather</u>, for example.   *Q40*

So, what we're going to do now is look at a short presentation in which you'll see all these tools . . .

TEST 2

PART 1

JUDY:	Good morning. Total Insurance. Judy speaking, how may I help you?
MICHAEL:	I recently shipped my belongings from overseas back here to Australia and I took out insurance with your company. Some items were damaged during the move so I need to make a claim. What do I have to do?
JUDY:	Okay, well first I need to get a few details about this. Can you give me your name please?
MICHAEL:	Yes. It's Michael Alexander.
JUDY:	Okay. And your address please?
MICHAEL:	My old address or my current one?
JUDY:	Your current one.
MICHAEL:	It's 24 Manly Street, Milperra near Sydney.
JUDY:	What was the suburb, sorry?
MICHAEL:	Milperra. <u>M-I-L-P-E-R-R-A</u>.
JUDY:	Right. Now, who was the shipping agent Mr Alexander?
MICHAEL:	You mean the company we used?
JUDY:	Yes, the company who packed everything up at the point of origin.
MICHAEL:	Oh, it was . . . er . . . <u>First Class Movers</u>.
JUDY:	Okay . . . where were the goods shipped from?
MICHAEL:	China, but the ship came via Singapore and was there for about a week.
JUDY:	Don't worry, all of that information will be in the documentation. Now, the dates. Do you know when the ship arrived?
MICHAEL:	It left on the 11th of October and got to Sydney on the <u>28th of November</u>.
JUDY:	Okay. I need one more thing. There's a reference number. It should be in the top right-hand corner of the pink form they gave you.

The Q markers appearing in the right margin: Q1 (at Milperra line), Q2 (at First Class Movers line), Q3 (at 28th of November line).

MICHAEL:	Let me have a look. I have so many papers. Yes, here it is. It's 601 ACK.
JUDY:	Thanks.

JUDY:	I need to take down a few details of the actual damage over the phone before you put in a full report. Can you tell me how many items were damaged and what the damage was?	
MICHAEL:	Yes, well four things actually. I'll start with the big things. My TV first of all. It's a large one . . . very expensive.	
JUDY:	Our insurance doesn't cover electrical problems.	
MICHAEL:	It isn't an electrical problem. <u>The screen has a huge crack</u> in it so it's unusable.	Q4
JUDY:	I see. Any idea of the price to repair it?	
MICHAEL:	No. Well, I don't think it can be repaired. <u>It will need a new one</u>.	Q4
JUDY:	Okay. I'll make a note of that and we'll see what we can do. Now, what was the second item?	
MICHAEL:	The cabinet from the <u>bathroom</u> was damaged as well. It's a lovely cabinet, we use it to keep our towels in.	Q5
JUDY:	And what is the extent of the damage?	
MICHAEL:	Well, the back and the sides seem okay but <u>the door has a huge hole in it</u>. It can't be repaired. I'm really not very happy about it.	Q6
JUDY:	And how much do you think it will cost to replace it?	
MICHAEL:	Well, when I bought it last year I paid $125 for it. But the one I've seen here in Sydney is a bit more expensive, it's <u>$140</u>.	Q7
JUDY:	Right, and what was the third item?	
MICHAEL:	My dining room table. It's a lovely table from Indonesia. It must have been very hot inside the container because one <u>leg has completely split</u> down the middle. The top and the other three look okay thank goodness.	Q8
JUDY:	Any idea of the price to repair it?	
MICHAEL:	Well, I had an estimate done on this actually because it is a very special table to us. They quoted us $200, which is really pricey so I hope the insurance will cover the total cost.	
JUDY:	I'm sure that will be fine. What was the last item, Mr Alexander?	
MICHAEL:	Well, we have a lovely set of china plates and dishes, you know, with matching cups, saucers, the lot. They were all in the one box which must have got dropped because some <u>plates</u> were broken – six actually.	Q9
JUDY:	And can you tell me the replacement value of these?	
MICHAEL:	Well, it's hard to say because they were part of a set but they can be up to $10 each as it's such a good set.	
JUDY:	Okay, so that would be around <u>$60</u> altogether?	Q10
MICHAEL:	Yes, that's right.	
JUDY:	And is that all of the items?	
MICHAEL:	Yes. So what do I have to do now?	

PART 2

Welcome to Green Vale Agricultural Park. As you know, we have only been open a week so you are amongst our first visitors. We have lots of fascinating indoor and outdoor exhibits on our huge complex, spreading hundreds of hectares. Our remit is <u>to give</u>   Q11 educational opportunities to the wider public as well as to offer research sites for a wide variety of agriculturists and other scientists.

Let's start by seeing what there is to do. As you can see here on our giant wall plan, we are now situated in the Reception block . . . here. As you walk out of the main door into the park there is a path you can follow. If you follow this route you will immediately come into the Rare Breeds section, where we keep a wide variety of animals which I shall be telling you a little more about later. Next to this . . . moving east . . . is the large grazing area for the rare breeds. Then further east . . . in the largest section of our Park is the <u>Forest</u> Area. *Q12* South of the grazing area and in fact just next to the Reception block is our Experimental Crop Area. In the middle of the Park . . . this circular area is our lake . . .. These two small rectangular shapes here . . . are the <u>Fish Farms</u> where we rear fish for sale. To the east of *Q13* those is the marsh area which attracts a great many migrant birds. In the south-eastern corner, beyond the marsh, is our <u>Market Garden</u> area, growing vegetables and flowers. *Q14*

All these areas can be visited by the general public for almost all the year . . . although . . . please take note of the large signs at the entrance to each area which tell. . . which tell you when certain areas are being used for particular controlled experiments and are therefore <u>temporarily out of bounds</u> to the public. *Q15*

You can see for yourself what a huge area the park covers and a key question is always, how can we move around? Well you have a choice of means . . . all environmentally friendly . . . cars are banned in the park. We have <u>bicycles</u> which you can hire behind the *Q16* Reception block . . . here . . . the healthy ones of you can go <u>on foot</u> and finally there's our <u>electric tram</u>, powered from solar cells. You find more information about this at the front entrance.

A good place to start on your tour is the Rare Breeds section. We keep <u>goats</u>, sheep and *Q17* <u>hens</u> and other kinds of poultry. We are also thinking of bringing in cows and horses but we do not, as yet, have facilities for these bigger animals. The animals are fed in public twice a day and a short lecture given on their feeding habits and nutritional needs. These are very popular with the public but of course we mustn't lose sight of the main purpose of having this section, not as such to preserve rare animals but <u>to maintain the diversity of breeds</u> to *Q18* broaden the gene pool for agricultural development. Green Vale changes with the seasons with different events happening at different times of the year. May will be perhaps our most spectacular month with the arrival of the Canada geese and when our fruit trees will be in full blossom, but there are interesting events on all year round . . . for example John Havers, <u>our expert fly fisherman, is currently giving displays</u> on the lake. Each of the *Q19* sections has its own seasonal calendar . . . please consult the summary board at the main entrance. And the final section, as we return to the Reception blocks, is the orchard.

Do take time to browse round our shop . . . there is a wide selection of <u>books on wildlife</u>, *Q20* some of them written by local authors, and the history of farming, including organic farming, something which the park will be diversifying into in the coming months.

PART 3

PROFESSOR: Good morning everyone. In today's seminar, Grant Freeman, a biologist who specialises in identifying insects, and who works for the Australian

	Quarantine Service, has come to talk to us about his current research work. Right, well, over to you, Grant.	
GRANT:	Good morning, everyone. I'm sure that you know that the quarantine service regulates all food brought into Australia. Well, obviously they want to protect Australia from diseases that might come in with imported goods, but they also want to prevent insect pests from being introduced into the country, and that's where I have a part to play. Anyway, my current research involves trying to find a particular type of bee, the Asian Honey Bee, and finding out whether there are any of them around in various states of Australia. We discovered a few of them in <u>Queensland</u> once and eradicated them. Now, we're pretty keen to make sure that there aren't any more getting in, particularly to New South Wales and other states.	*Q21*
STUDENT 1:	What's wrong with Asian Honey Bees? Are they so different from Australian bees?	
GRANT:	Well, in fact, they look almost the same, but <u>they are infested with mites</u> – microscopic creatures which live on them, and which can seriously damage our own home-grown bees, or could even wipe them out.	*Q22*
PROFESSOR:	Well, what would happen if Australian bees died out?	
GRANT:	Well, the honey from Australian bees is of excellent quality, much better than the stuff the Asian bees produce. In fact, <u>Australia exports native Queen bees to a large number of countries because of this</u>. When the European Honey Bee was first discovered out in the bush, we found they made really unpleasant honey and they were also too big to pollinate many of our native flowers here in Australia.	*Q23*
STUDENT 2:	That must have had a devastating effect on the natural flora. Did you lose any species?	
GRANT:	No, we managed to get them under control before that happened but if Asian bees got in there could be other consequences. <u>We could lose a lot of money</u> because you might not be aware, but it's estimated that native bees' pollination of flower and vegetable crops is worth 1.2 billion dollars a year. So in a way they're the farmers' friend. Oh, and another thing is, if you're stung by an Asian Honey Bee, it can produce an allergic reaction in some people; so they're much more dangerous than native bees.	*Q24*

PROFESSOR:	How will you know if Asian bees have entered Australia?	
GRANT:	We're looking at the diet of the bird called the Rainbow Bee Eater. The Bee Eater <u>doesn't care what it eats, as long as they're insects</u>. But the interesting thing about this bird is that we are able to analyse exactly what it eats and that's really helpful if we're looking for introduced insects.	*Q25*
PROFESSOR:	How come?	
GRANT:	Because insects have their skeletons outside their bodies, so the Bee Eaters digest the meat from the inside. Then they bring up all the indigestible bits of skeleton and, of course, the wings in a pellet – a small ball of waste material which they cough up.	
PROFESSOR:	That sounds a bit unpleasant. So, how do you go about it?	
GRANT:	In the field we track down the Bee Eaters and find their favourite <u>feeding</u> spots, you know, the places where the birds usually feed. It's here that we can find the pellets. We collect them up and take them back to the <u>laboratory</u> to examine the contents.	*Q26* *Q27*

PROFESSOR:	How do you do that?
GRANT:	The pellets are really hard, especially if they have been out in the sun for a few days so, first of all, we treat them by adding water to moisten them and make them softer. Then we pull them apart under the microscope. Everything's all scrunched up but we're looking for wings so we just pull them all out and straighten them. Then we identify them to see if we can find any Asian bee wings.
PROFESSOR:	And how many have you found?
GRANT:	So far our research shows that Asian bees have not entered Australia in any number – it's a good result and much more reliable than trying to find live ones as evidence of introduced insects.
PROFESSOR:	Well, that's fascinating! Thank you, Grant, for those insights. I hope that you might inspire some of our students here to conduct some similar experiments.

Q28 (beside "water")
Q29 (beside "wings")
Q30 (beside "reliable")

PART 4

I've been doing some research into what people in Britain think of doctors, the ones who work in general practice – the first call for medical care – and comparing this with the situation in a couple of other countries. I want to talk about the rationale behind what I decided to do.

Now I had to set up my programme of research in three different countries so I approached postgraduates in my field in overseas departments, contacting them by email, to organise   Q31
things for me at their end. I thought I would have trouble recruiting help but in fact everyone was very willing and sometimes their tutors got involved too.

I had to give my helpers clear instructions about what kind of sample population I wanted them to use. I decided that people under 18 should be excluded because most of them are students or looking for their first job, and also I decided at this stage just to focus on men   Q32
who were in employment, and set up something for people who didn't have jobs and for employed women later on as a separate investigation.

I specifically wanted to do a questionnaire, and interviews with a focus group. With the questionnaire, rather than limiting it to one specific point, I wanted to include as much   Q33
variety as possible. I know questionnaires are a very controlled way to do things but I thought I could do taped interviews later on to counteract the effects of this. And the focus group may also prove useful in future, by targeting subjects I can easily return to, as the participants tend to be more involved.

So I'm just collating the results now. At the moment it looks as if, in the UK, despite the fact   Q34
that newspapers continually report that people are unhappy with medical care, in fact it is mainly the third level of care, which takes place in hospitals, that they are worried about. Government reforms have been proposed at all levels and although their success is not guaranteed, long-term hospital care is in fact probably less of an issue than the media would have us believe. However, I've still got quite a bit of data to look at.

Certainly I will need to do more far-reaching research than I had anticipated in order to   Q35
establish if people want extra medical staff invested in the community, or if they want care to revert to fewer, but larger, key medical units. The solution may well be something that

can be easily implemented by those responsible in local government, with central government support of course.

This first stage has proved very valuable though. I was surprised by how willing most of the subjects were to get involved in the project – I had expected some unwillingness to answer questions honestly. But I was taken aback and rather concerned that something I thought I'd set up very well didn't necessarily seem that way to everyone in my own department.   *Q36*

I thought you might also be interested in some of the problems I encountered in collecting my data. There were odd cases that threw me – one of the subjects who I had approached while he was out shopping in town, decided to pull out when it came to the second round. It   *Q37* was a shame as it was someone who I would like to have interviewed more closely.

And one of the first-year students I interviewed wanted reassurance that no names would   *Q38* be traceable from the answers. I was so surprised, because they think nothing of telling you about themselves and their opinions in seminar groups!

Then, one of the people that I work with got a bit funny. The questions were quite personal and one minute he said he'd do it, then the next day he wouldn't, and in the end he did do   *Q39* it. It's hard not to get angry in that situation but I tried to keep focused on the overall picture in order to stay calm.

The most bizarre case was a telephone interview I did with a teacher at a university in France. He answered all my questions in great detail – but then when I asked how much access he had to dangerous substances he wouldn't tell me exactly what his work involved.   *Q40* It's a real eye-opener . . .

TEST 3

PART 1

WOMAN:	Good morning. How can I help you?
MAN:	Hello. I'm interested in renting a house somewhere in the town.
WOMAN:	Right. Could I have your name please?
MAN:	Yes, it's Steven Godfrey.
WOMAN:	And tell me how many bedrooms you're looking for.
MAN:	Well, we'd need four, because I'm going to share the house with three friends.
WOMAN:	Okay, there are several of that size on our books. They mostly belong to families who are working abroad at the moment. What about the location?
MAN:	It'd be nice to be central.

Q1

WOMAN:	That might be difficult, as most houses of that size are in the suburbs. Still, there are a few. What's your upper limit for the rent?
MAN:	We'd like something around £500 a month, but we could go up to £600 if we have to. But we can't go beyond that.

Q2

WOMAN:	Do you know how long you want to rent the house for? The minimum let is six months, as you probably realise.

MAN:	We're at college here for <u>two years</u>, and we don't want to have to move during that time if we can avoid it.	*Q3*
WOMAN:	Right. And how soon do you want to move in? All our lets start on the first of the month.	
MAN:	Well, as soon as possible, really, so that means September 1st.	
WOMAN:	Okay, let me have a look at what we've got . . .. We have photographs of all the houses on our books, so you can get an idea of what they're like. There's this one in Oakington Avenue, at £550 a month. Combined living room and dining room, with a separate kitchen. It doesn't have a <u>garage</u>, though you can park in the road.	*Q4*
MAN:	Ah, we'd prefer to have one, if possible.	
WOMAN:	Right. Then have a look at this house, in Mead Street. It's got a very large living room and kitchen, bathroom, cloakroom . . .	
MAN:	How much is it?	
WOMAN:	That one's 580. It's very well furnished and equipped. It also has plenty of space for parking, and it's available for a minimum of a year. Oh, and there's a big <u>garden</u>.	*Q5*
MAN:	I don't think we could cope with that, to be honest. We'll be too busy to look after it.	
WOMAN:	Okay. Then there's this older house in Hamilton Road: living room, kitchen-diner, and it has a <u>study</u>. 550 a month.	*Q6*
MAN:	That looks rather nice. But whereabouts in Hamilton Road?	
WOMAN:	Towards the western end.	
MAN:	Oh, that'll be very <u>noisy</u>. I know the area.	*Q7*
WOMAN:	Yes, it's pretty lively. Some people like it, though. Well, what about this house in Devon Close?	
MAN:	That looks lovely.	
WOMAN:	There's a big demand for houses in that area, so prices tend to be quite high. But this one hasn't been decorated for a few years, which has kept the rent down a bit. It's got a living room, dining room and small kitchen, and it's <u>595</u> a month. I think it would suit you, from what you've said.	*Q8*
MAN:	It sounds fine.	

MAN:	Why's that part of town so popular?	
WOMAN:	Well, there's a big scheme to improve the district, and it'll soon have the best facilities for miles around.	
MAN:	What sort of thing?	
WOMAN:	There's a big sports centre under construction, which will be very impressive when it's finished. In fact <u>the swimming pool's already opened</u>, ahead of schedule, and it's attracting a lot of people.	*Q9 & 10*
MAN:	What about cinemas: are there any in the area?	
WOMAN:	The only one closed down last year, and it's now in the process of being converted into a film museum. The local people are trying to get a new cinema added to the scheme.	
MAN:	I think I heard something about a plan to replace <u>the existing concert hall</u> with a larger one.	*Q9 & 10*

WOMAN:	Ah, that's due to start next year.
MAN:	Well it sounds an interesting area to live in. Could I go and see the house, please?
WOMAN:	Yes, of course.

PART 2

Hello, and welcome to *Focus on the Arts*. I'm your host – Dave Green – and this is your very own local radio programme. Every Friday evening we put the spotlight on different arts and culture facilities, and look at the shows and events that are on offer in the coming week.

And today the focus is on The National Arts Centre. Now, if you don't already know it yourself, I'm sure you've all heard of it. It's famous throughout the world <u>as one of the major</u>   Q11
<u>venues for classical music</u>.

But did you know that it is actually much more than just a place to hear concerts? The Centre itself is a huge complex that caters for a great range of arts. Under a single roof it houses concert rooms, theatres, cinemas, art galleries and a wonderful public library, as well as service facilities including three restaurants and a <u>bookshop</u>. So at any one time,   Q12
the choice of entertainment there is simply enormous.

So, how did they manage to build such a big arts complex right in the heart of the city? Well, the area was completely destroyed by bombs during the war in 1940. So the opportunity was taken to create a cultural centre that would be, what they called: 'the City's gift to the Nation'. Of course it took a while for such a big project to get started, but it was <u>planned</u> in the 60s, built in the 70s and eventually opened to the public in <u>1983</u>. Ever since   Q13 & 14
then it has proved to be a great success. It is not privately owned, like many arts centres, but is still in public hands – it's run by the <u>City Council</u>. Both our National Symphony   Q15
Orchestra and National Theatre Company were involved in the planning of the project, and they are now based there – giving regular performances every week – and as the Centre is open <u>363</u> days of the year, there are plenty of performances to choose from.   Q16

So, to give you some idea of what's on, and to help you choose from the many possibilities, we've made a selection of the star attractions.

If you're interested in classical music, then we recommend you go along to the National on either Monday or Tuesday evening at 7.30 for a spectacular production of 'The Magic Flute' – probably the most popular of all Mozart's operas. It's in <u>the Garden Hall</u> and tickets start   Q17
at only £8.00, but you'll have to be early if you want to get them that cheap! And remember, it's only on for those two evenings.

For those more interested in the cinema, you might like to see the new Canadian film which is showing on Wednesday evening at 8pm in Cinema 2. And that's called <u>'Three Lives.'</u> It's   Q18
had fantastic reviews and tickets cost just <u>£4.50</u>, which is a reduction on the usual price of   Q19
£5.50. So, it's really good value, especially for such a great movie.

But you can see the centre's *main* attraction at the weekend, because on Saturday and Sunday, 11 am to 10 pm, they're showing a wonderful new exhibition that hasn't been seen anywhere else in Europe yet. It's a collection of Chinese Art called <u>'Faces of China'</u> – that's   Q20 in Gallery 1 – and it has some really fascinating paintings and sculptures by leading artists from all over China – and the good news is that it is completely free, so don't miss it!

So why not go along to the National Arts Centre next week for one – or all – of these great events – and you can always pick up a programme and check out all the other performances and exhibitions on offer, or coming soon, on almost every day of the year.

Next week we'll be looking at the new Museum of Science . . .

PART 3

WOMAN:	I've been reading your personal statement, Paul. First, let's talk about your work experience in South America. What took you there? Was it to gain more fluency in Spanish?
PAUL:	Well, as I'm combining Spanish with Latin American studies, my main idea was <u>to find out more about the way people lived there</u>. My spoken Spanish was already pretty good in fact.

Q21

WOMAN:	So you weren't too worried about language barriers?
PAUL:	No. In fact, I ended up teaching English there, although that wasn't my original choice of work.
WOMAN:	I see. How did you find out about all this?
PAUL:	I found an agency that runs all kinds of voluntary projects in South America.
WOMAN:	What kind of work?
PAUL:	Well, there were several possibilities.
WOMAN:	You mean construction? Engineering work?
PAUL:	Yes, getting involved in building projects was an option. Then there was <u>tourism – taking tourists for walks around the volcanoes – which I actually chose to do</u>, and then there was work with local farmers.

Q22

WOMAN:	But you didn't continue with that project. Why not?
PAUL:	Because I never really knew whether I'd be needed or not. I'd thought it might be difficult physically, but I was certainly fit enough . . . no, <u>I wanted to do something that had more of a proper structure to it</u>, I suppose. I get de-motivated otherwise.

Q23

WOMAN:	What do you think you learned from your experience? It must have been a great opportunity to examine community life.
PAUL:	Yes, but it was difficult at first to be accepted by the locals. It was a very remote village and some of them were reluctant to speak to me – although they were always interested in my clothes and how much I'd had to pay for them.
WOMAN:	Well, that's understandable.
PAUL:	Yes, but things soon improved. <u>What struck me was that when people became more comfortable with me and less suspicious</u>, we really connected with each other in a meaningful way.

Q24

WOMAN:	You made good friends?
PAUL:	Yes, with two of the families in particular.
WOMAN:	Good. What about management. Did you have a project manager?
PAUL:	Yes and <u>he gave me lots of advice and guidance</u>.

Q25

WOMAN:	And was he good at managing too?

PAUL:	That wasn't his strong point! I think he was often more interested in the academic side of things than filing reports. He was a bit of a dreamer.
WOMAN:	And did you have a contract?
PAUL:	I had to stay for a minimum of three months. My parents were surprised when I asked to stay longer – six months in the end. I was so happy there.
WOMAN:	And did anything on the administration side of things surprise you? What was the food and lodging like?
PAUL:	Simple . . . but there was plenty to eat and I only paid seven dollars a day for that which was amazing really. And they gave me all the equipment I needed . . . <u>even a laptop</u>.
WOMAN:	<u>You didn't expect that then</u>?
PAUL:	<u>No</u>.
WOMAN:	Well, I'll look forward to hearing more.

Q26

WOMAN:	But now let's look at these modules. You'll need to start thinking about which ones you'll definitely want to study. The first one here is Gender Studies in Latin America.
PAUL:	Mmm . . .
WOMAN:	It looks at how gender analysis is reconfiguring civil society in Latin America. Women are increasingly occupying positions in government and in other elected leadership positions in Latin America. I think you'd find it interesting.
PAUL:	<u>If it was to do with people in the villages rather than those in the public sphere, I would</u>.
WOMAN:	Okay. What about Second Language Acquisition?
PAUL:	Do you think I'd find that useful?
WOMAN:	Well, you've had some practical experience in the field, I think it would be.
PAUL:	I hadn't thought about that. <u>I'll put that down as a definite, then</u>.
WOMAN:	Okay. What about Indigenous Women's Lives. That sounds appropriate.
PAUL:	I thought so too, but I looked at last year's exam questions and that changed my mind.
WOMAN:	Don't judge the value of the course on that. Maybe, talk to some other students first <u>and we can talk about it again later</u>.
PAUL:	<u>Okay</u>.
WOMAN:	Yes. And lastly, will you sign up for Portuguese lessons?
PAUL:	My Spanish is good, so would I find that module easy?
WOMAN:	Not necessarily. Some people find that Spanish interferes with learning Portuguese . . . getting the accent right too. It's quite different in a lot of ways.
PAUL:	<u>Well, I'd much sooner do something else, then</u>.
WOMAN:	Alright. Now, what we need to do is . . .

Q27

Q28

Q29

Q30

PART 4

Good morning, everyone. In the last few lectures I've been dealing with business finance, but now I'm going to move on to business systems. And in today's lecture I'm going to talk about what can go wrong when businesses try to copy their own best practices.

Once a business has successfully introduced a new process – managing a branch bank, say, or selling a new product – the parent organisation naturally wants to repeat that success, and capture it if possible on a bigger scale. The goal, then, is to utilise existing knowledge and not to generate new knowledge. It's a less glamorous activity than pure innovation, but it actually happens more often, as a matter of fact. However, surprisingly, getting things right the second time is not necessarily any simpler than it was the first time. *Q31*

Now, there's been a lot of research into how companies can repeat their previous successes, and it certainly hasn't been confined to the United States. It seems that most large industries are trying to repeat their own successes, and manage the knowledge they've acquired – but even so it has been shown that the overwhelming majority of attempts fail. A host of studies confirm this, covering a wide range of business settings: branch banks, retail stores, real estate agencies, factories, call centres . . . to name but a few. *Q32*

So why do so few managers get things right the second or third time? Let's consider one reason for failure – placing too much trust in the people who are running the successful operation, the 'experts' shall we say. Managers who want to apply existing knowledge typically start off by going to an expert – such as the person who designed and is running a successful department store – and picking their brains. Now, this approach can be used if you want to gain a rough understanding of a particular system, or understand smaller, isolated problems. The trouble is, even the expert doesn't fully grasp the whole thing because when it comes to complex systems, the individual components of the process are interwoven with one another. The expert never has complete access to the necessary information. And the situation's complicated even further by the fact that experts are usually not aware of their own ignorance. The ignorance can take various forms. For instance, a lot of details of the system are invisible to managers. Some may be difficult to describe – learned on the job and well known by workers perhaps, but impossible to describe in a way that's helpful. And there are some things that people know or do that they're not even aware of. *Q33* *Q34*

Now, let's consider two types of mistake that can occur when a manager actually starts to set up a duplicate system to replicate a successful process. Firstly, perhaps he forgets that he was just trying to copy another process, and starts trying to improve on it. Another mistake is trying to use the best parts of various different systems, in the hope of creating the perfect combination. *Q35*

Unfortunately, attempts like these usually turn out to be misguided and lead to problems. Why? Well, for various reasons. Perhaps there weren't really any advantages after all, because the information wasn't accurate. Or perhaps the business settings weren't really comparable. More typically, the advantages are real enough, but there are also disadvantages that have been overlooked. For example, the modifications might compromise safety in some way. *Q36*

So, what's the solution? Well, I don't intend to suggest that it's easy to get things right the second time . . . it's not. But the underlying problem has more to do with attitudes than the actual difficulty of the task, and there are ways of getting it right. These involve adjusting attitudes, first of all . . . being more realistic and cautious really. Secondly, they involve exerting strict controls on the organisational and operational systems. And this in turn means copying the original as closely as possible. Not merely duplicating the physical *Q37* *Q38*

characteristics of the <u>factory</u>, but also duplicating the <u>skills</u> that the original employees had.　　*Q39 & 40*
Reliance on a template like this offers the huge advantage of built-in consistency.

TEST 4

PART 1

WOMAN:	Hello, West Bay Hotel. Can I help you?	
MAN:	Oh, good morning. I'm ringing about your advertisement in the Evening Gazette.	
WOMAN:	Is that the one for temporary staff?	
MAN:	That's right.	
WOMAN:	Yes. I'm afraid the person who's dealing with that isn't in today, but I can give you the main details if you like.	
MAN:	Yes please. Could you tell me what kind of staff you are looking for?	
WOMAN:	We're looking for <u>waiters</u> at the moment. There was one post for a cook, but that's already been taken.	*Q1*
MAN:	Oh right. Erm, what are the hours of work?	
WOMAN:	There are two different shifts – there's a day shift from 7 to 2 and a late shift from 4 till 11.	
MAN:	And can people choose which one they want to do?	
WOMAN:	Not normally, because everyone would choose the day shift I suppose. You alternate from one week to another.	
MAN:	Okay. I'm just writing all this down. What about time off?	
WOMAN:	<u>You get one day off and I think you can negotiate which one you want, it's more or less up to you.</u> But it has to be the same one every week.	*Q2*
MAN:	Do you know what the rates of pay are?	
WOMAN:	Yes, I've got them here. You get £5.50 an hour, and that includes a <u>break</u>.	*Q3*
MAN:	Do I have to go home to eat or . . .	
WOMAN:	You don't have to. <u>You can get a meal in the hotel</u> if you want to, and there's no charge for it so you might as well.	*Q4*
MAN:	Oh good. Yes, so let's see. I'd get er, two hundred and twenty one, no, two hundred and thirty one pounds a week?	
WOMAN:	You'd also get tips – our guests tend to be quite generous.	

MAN:	Erm, is there a uniform? What about clothes?	
WOMAN:	Yes, I forgot to mention that. You need to wear a white shirt, just a plain one, and <u>dark</u> trousers. You know, not green or anything like that. And we don't supply those.	*Q5*
MAN:	That's okay, I've got trousers, I'd just have to buy a couple of shirts. What about anything else? Do I need a waistcoat or anything?	
WOMAN:	You have to wear <u>a jacket, but the hotel lends you that.</u>	*Q6*
MAN:	I see. Er, one last thing – I don't know what the starting date is.	
WOMAN:	Just a minute, I think it's some time <u>around the end of June. Yes, the 28th,</u> in time for the summer.	*Q7*
MAN:	That's great. I'm available from the 10th.	

WOMAN:	Oh good. Well, if you can call again you need to speak to the Service Manager. Her name's Jane Urwin, that's U-R-W-I-N, and she'll probably arrange to meet you.	*Q8*
MAN:	Okay. And when's the best time to ring?	
WOMAN:	Could you call tomorrow? Um, she usually starts checking the rooms at midday, so before then if you can, so she'll have more time to chat. I'll just give you her number because she's got a direct line.	*Q9*
MAN:	Thanks.	
WOMAN:	It's 832 double-0 9.	
MAN:	823 double-0 9?	
WOMAN:	832.	
MAN:	Oh, okay. Yes, I'll do that.	
WOMAN:	And by the way, she will ask you for a reference, so you might like to be thinking about that. You know, just someone who knows you and can vouch for you.	*Q10*
MAN:	Yes, no problem. Well, thanks very much for your help.	
WOMAN:	You're welcome. Bye.	
MAN:	Bye.	

PART 2

CAROL:	Good morning and welcome again to *Your City Today.* With me today is Graham Campbell, a councillor from the city council. He will be telling us about the plan to improve the fast-growing suburb of Red Hill. Good morning Graham and welcome to the show.	
GRAHAM:	Good morning, Carol.	
CAROL:	Now, Graham, I understand that there has been a lot of community consultation for the new plan?	
GRAHAM:	Yes, we've tried to address some of the concerns that local groups told us about. People we've heard from are mainly worried about traffic in the area, and, in particular, the increasing speed of cars near schools. They feel that it is only a matter of time before there is an accident as a lot of the children walk to the school. So we're trying to do something about that. Another area of concern is the overhead power lines. These are very old and a lot of people we spoke to asked if something could be done about them. Well, I'm happy to report that the power company have agreed to move the power lines underground at a cost of $800,000. I think that will really improve the look of the area, as well as being safer.	*Q11* *Q12*
CAROL:	That's good to know, but will that mean an increase in rates for the local businesses in that area?	
GRAHAM:	Well, the power company have agreed to bear the cost of this themselves after a lot of discussion with the council. This is wonderful news as the council now has some extra funds for us to put into other things like tree planting and art work.	*Q13*

| GRAHAM: | Now, we've also put together a map which we've sent out to all the residents in the area. And on the map we've marked the proposed changes. Firstly, we'll plant mature pine trees to provide shelter and shade just to the right of the supermarket in Days Road. In order to address the traffic | *Q14* |

problems, the pavements <u>on the corner of Carberry and Thomas Street will</u>   *Q15*
<u>be widened</u>. This will help to reduce the speed of vehicles entering Thomas
Street. We think it's very important to separate the local residential streets
from the main road. <u>So the roadway at the entry to Thomas Street from</u>   *Q16*
<u>Days Road will be painted red</u>. This should mark it more clearly and act as
a signal for traffic to slow down. One way of making sure that the
pedestrians are safe is to increase signage at the intersections. A 'keep
clear' sign will be erected <u>at the junction of Evelyn Street and Hill Street</u>, to   *Q17*
enable traffic to exit at all times. Something we're planning to do to help
control the flow of traffic in the area is <u>to install traffic lights half way down</u>   *Q18*
<u>Hill Street where it crosses Days Road</u>. Now, we haven't only thought about
the cars and traffic, of course, there's also something for the children. We're
going to get school children in the area to research a local story, the life of a
local sports hero perhaps, and an artist will incorporate that story into
paintings <u>on the wall of a building on the other side of Hill Street from the</u>   *Q19*
<u>supermarket</u>. And finally, we've agreed to build a new children's playground
which will be <u>at the other end of Hill Street close to the intersection with</u>   *Q20*
<u>Carberry Street</u>.

CAROL:	Wonderful, now, what's the next stage?
GRAHAM:	Well, the final plan . . .

PART 3

DAN:	Hi Jeannie. How's it going?
JEANNIE:	Oh, hello Dan. Pretty well, thanks. Have you managed to get the money for the course yet?
DAN:	Yes, that's all sorted out now, thanks. It took long enough, though. It was practically a year ago that I applied to my local council for a grant, and it took them six months to turn me down.
JEANNIE:	That's really slow.
DAN:	And I thought I was eligible for government funding, but it seems I was mistaken. So then I asked the boss of the company I used to work for if they would sponsor me, and much to my surprise, <u>he said they'd make a</u> <u>contribution.</u> *Q21 & 22*
JEANNIE:	But what about college grants and scholarships? There must be some you could apply for.
DAN:	Yes, there are, but they're all so small that I decided to leave them until I was desperate.
JEANNIE:	Uhuh.
DAN:	And in fact I didn't need to apply. My parents had been saying that as I already had a job, I ought to support myself through college. <u>But in the</u> <u>end they took pity on me, so now I've just about got enough</u>. *Q21 & 22*
JEANNIE:	That's good.
DAN:	So now I can put a bit of effort into meeting people – I haven't had time so far. Any suggestions?
JEANNIE:	What about joining some college clubs?
DAN:	Oh right. You joined several didn't you?

JEANNIE:	Yes, I'm in the drama club. It's our first performance next week, so we're rehearsing frantically, and I've got behind with my work, but it's worth it. I'm hoping to be in the spring production, too.
DAN:	I've never liked acting. Are you doing anything else?
JEANNIE:	I enjoyed singing when I was at school, so I joined a group when I came to college. <u>I don't think the conductor stretches us enough</u>, though so I'll give up after the next concert. And I also joined the debating society. It's fun, <u>but with all the rehearsing I'm doing, something has to go</u>, and I'm afraid that's the one.
DAN:	Do you do any sports?
JEANNIE:	Yes, I'm in one of the hockey teams. I'm not very good, but I'd really miss it if I stopped. I decided to try tennis when I came to college, and I'm finding it pretty tough going. I'm simply not fit enough.
DAN:	Nor me. I think I'll give that a miss!
JEANNIE:	I'm hoping it'll help me to build up my stamina, but it'll probably be a long haul.
DAN:	Good luck.
JEANNIE:	Thanks.
DAN:	How are you finding the course?
JEANNIE:	I wish we had more seminars.
DAN:	What? I'd have thought we had more than enough already. All those people saying clever things that I could never think of – it's quite interesting, but <u>I wonder if I'm clever enough</u> to be doing this course.
JEANNIE:	I find it helpful to listen to the other people. I like the way we're exploring the subject, and working towards getting insight into it.
DAN:	How do you get on with your tutor? I don't think I'm on the same wavelength as mine, so I feel I'm not getting anything out of the tutorials. It would be more productive to read a book instead.
JEANNIE:	Oh, mine's very demanding. She gives me lots of feedback and advice, <u>so I've got much better at writing essays. And she's helping me plan my revision</u> for the end-of-year exams.
DAN:	Do tell me, I always struggle with revision.

Q23 & 24

Q23 & 24

Q25

Q26

JEANNIE:	Well, the first thing is to find out exactly what's required in the exams.
DAN:	Mm. Would it help to get hold of some past papers?
JEANNIE:	Yes. They'll help to make it clear.
DAN:	Right, I'll do that. Then what?
JEANNIE:	Then you can sort out your revision <u>priorities</u>, based on what's most likely to come up. I put these on a card, and read them through regularly.
DAN:	Uhuh.
JEANNIE:	But that isn't enough in itself. You also need a <u>timetable</u>, to see how you can fit everything in, in the time available. Then keep it in front of you while you're studying.
DAN:	I've done that before, but it hasn't helped me!
JEANNIE:	Maybe you need to do something different every day, so if you break down your revision into <u>small tasks</u>, and allocate them to specific days, there's more incentive to tackle them. With big topics you're more likely to put off starting.

Q27

Q28

Q29

DAN:	Good idea.
JEANNIE:	And as I revise each topic I write a <u>single paragraph</u> about it – then later I can read it through quickly, and it helps fix things in my mind.
DAN:	That's brilliant.
JEANNIE:	I also write answers to questions for the exam practice. It's hard to make myself do it, though!
DAN:	Well, I'll try. Thanks a lot, Jeannie. That's a great help.
JEANNIE:	No problem.
DAN:	See you around.
JEANNIE:	Bye.

Q30 is marked beside the JEANNIE line beginning "And as I revise each topic".

PART 4

Good morning, everyone. I've been invited to talk about my research project into Australian Aboriginal rock paintings. The Australian Aborigines have recorded both real and symbolic images of their time on rock walls for many thousands of years. Throughout the long history of this tradition, new images have appeared and new painting styles have developed. And these characteristics can be used to categorise the different artistic styles. Among these are what we call the Dynamic, Yam and Modern styles of painting.

One of the most significant characteristics of the different styles is the way that humans are depicted in the paintings. The more recent paintings show people in static poses. But the first human images to dominate rock art paintings, over 8,000 years ago, were full of movement. These paintings showed people hunting and cooking food and so they were given the name 'Dynamic' to reflect this energy. It's quite amazing considering they were painted in such a simple stick-like form. In the Yam period, there was a movement away from stick figures to a more naturalistic shape. However, they didn't go as far as the <u>Modern style, which is known as 'x-ray' because it actually makes a feature of the internal skeleton</u> as well as the organs of animals and humans. <u>The Yam style of painting got its name from the fact that it featured much curvier figures</u> that actually resemble the vegetable called a yam, which is similar to a sweet potato. <u>The Modern paintings are interesting because they include paintings at the time of the first contact with European settlers. Aborigines managed to convey the idea of the settlers' clothing by simply painting the Europeans without any hands</u>, indicating the habit of standing with their hands in their pockets! Size is another characteristic. The more recent images tend to be life size or even larger, but the <u>Dynamic figures are painted in miniature.</u>   *Q34*

Aboriginal rock art also records the environmental changes that occurred over thousands of years. For example, we know from the Dynamic paintings that over 8,000 years ago, Aborigines would have rarely eaten fish and sea levels were much lower at this time. In fact, <u>fish didn't start to appear in paintings until the Yam period along with shells and other marine images. The paintings of the Yam tradition also suggest that, during this time, the Aborigines moved away from animals as their main food source and began including vegetables in their diet, as these feature prominently.</u> Freshwater creatures didn't appear in the paintings until the Modern period from 4,000 years ago.

Q31, Q32, Q33 are marked beside the second paragraph; Q35, Q36 beside the final paragraph.

So, these paintings have already taught us a lot. But one image that has always intrigued us is known as the 'Rainbow Serpent'. The Rainbow Serpent, which is the focus of my most recent project, gets its name from its snake or serpent-like body and it first appeared in the Yam period 4 to 6,000 years ago. Many believe it is a curious mixture of kangaroo, snake and crocodile. But we decided to study the Rainbow Serpent paintings to see if we could locate the <u>animal</u> that the very first painters based their image on.   *Q37*

The Yam period coincided with the end of the last ice age. This brought about tremendous change in the environment, with the <u>sea levels rising</u> and creeping steadily inland. This   *Q38* flooded many familiar land features and also caused a great deal of disruption to traditional patterns of life, <u>hunting</u> in particular. New shores were formed and totally different creatures *Q39* would have washed up onto the shores. We studied 107 paintings of the Rainbow Serpent and found that the one creature that matches it most closely was the Ribboned Pipefish, which is a type of sea horse. This sea creature would have been a totally unfamiliar sight in the inland regions where the image is found and may have been the inspiration behind the early paintings.

So, at the end of the ice age there would have been enormous changes in animal and plant life. It's not surprising then, that the Aborigines linked this abundance to the new creatures they witnessed. Even today, Aborigines see the Rainbow Serpent as a symbol of <u>creation</u>,   *Q40* which is understandable given the increase in vegetation and the new life forms that featured when the image first appeared.

Listening and Reading Answer Keys

TEST 1

LISTENING

PART 1, Questions 1–10

1	C
2	B
3	48 North Avenue
4	WS6 2YH
5	01674 553242
6	(free) drink(s)/refreshment(s)
7	(the/a) pianist/piano player
8	10.50
9	4
10	50%

PART 2, Questions 11–20

11	1.30
12	25 December/Christmas Day
13	car-park/parking lot
14	45
15	(some) tables
16–18	**IN ANY ORDER**
	C
	F
	G
19&20	**IN EITHER ORDER**
	B
	E

PART 3, Questions 21–30

21	A
22	C
23	A
24	B
25–27	**IN ANY ORDER**
	B
	C
	F
28	12,000
29	horses
30	caves

PART 4, Questions 31–40

31	surface
32	environment
33	impact(s)/effect(s)
34	urban
35	problems
36	images
37	patterns
38	distortion(s)
39	traffic
40	weather

If you score . . .

0–14	15–29	30–40
you are unlikely to get an acceptable score under examination conditions and we recommend that you spend a lot of time improving your English before you take IELTS.	you may get an acceptable score under examination conditions but we recommend that you think about having more practice or lessons before you take IELTS.	you are likely to get an acceptable score under examination conditions but remember that different institutions will find different scores acceptable.

ACADEMIC READING

Reading Passage 1, Questions 1–13

1 D
2 B
3 F
4 E
5 B
6 F
7 D
8 A
9 (ship's) anchor/(an/the) anchor
10 (escape) wheel
11 tooth
12 (long) pendulum
13 second

Reading Passage 2, Questions 14–26

14 ii
15 iii
16 v
17 iv
18 viii
19 vii
20 FALSE
21 FALSE
22 NOT GIVEN
23 TRUE
24 TRUE
25 FALSE
26 TRUE

Reading Passage 3, Questions 27–40

27 E
28 B
29 A
30 F
31 sender
32 picture/image
33 receiver
34&35 *IN EITHER ORDER*
        sensory leakage (or)
        (outright) fraud
36 computers
37 human involvement
38 meta-analysis
39 lack of consistency
40 big/large enough

If you score . . .

0–12	13–29	30–40
you are unlikely to get an acceptable score under examination conditions and we recommend that you spend a lot of time improving your English before you take IELTS.	you may get an acceptable score under examination conditions but we recommend that you think about having more practice or lessons before you take IELTS.	you are likely to get an acceptable score under examination conditions but remember that different institutions will find different scores acceptable.

TEST 2

LISTENING

PART 1, Questions 1–10

1	Milperra
2	First Class Movers
3	28 November
4	screen
5	bathroom
6	door
7	140
8	leg
9	plates
10	60

PART 2, Questions 11–20

11	B
12	(the) Forest
13	Fish Farm(s)
14	Market Garden
15	C
16	A
17	C
18	B
19	C
20	A

PART 3, Questions 21–30

21	A
22	B
23	C
24	A
25	insects
26	feeding/eating
27	laboratory
28	water
29	wings
30	reliable/accurate

PART 4, Questions 31–40

31	B
32	B
33	A
34	A
35	C
36	C
37	B
38	F
39	D
40	C

If you score . . .

0–13	14–27	28–40
you are unlikely to get an acceptable score under examination conditions and we recommend that you spend a lot of time improving your English before you take IELTS.	you may get an acceptable score under examination conditions but we recommend that you think about having more practice or lessons before you take IELTS.	you are likely to get an acceptable score under examination conditions but remember that different institutions will find different scores acceptable.

ACADEMIC READING

Reading Passage 1, Questions 1–13

1	spinning
2	(perfectly) unblemished
3	labour/labor-intensive
4	thickness
5	marked
6	(molten) glass
7	(molten) tin/metal
8	rollers
9	TRUE
10	NOT GIVEN
11	FALSE
12	TRUE
13	TRUE

Reading Passage 2, Questions 14–26

14	ii
15	vii
16	ix
17	iv
18&19	**IN EITHER ORDER**
	C
	B
20	A
21	H
22	G
23	C
24	C
25	A
26	B

Reading Passage 3, Questions 27–40

27	viii
28	ii
29	vi
30	i
31	iii
32	v
33	C
34	A
35	C
36	D
37	clothing
38	vocabulary
39	chemicals
40	cultures

If you score . . .

0–11	12–28	29–40
you are unlikely to get an acceptable score under examination conditions and we recommend that you spend a lot of time improving your English before you take IELTS.	you may get an acceptable score under examination conditions but we recommend that you think about having more practice or lessons before you take IELTS.	you are likely to get an acceptable score under examination conditions but remember that different institutions will find different scores acceptable.

TEST 3

LISTENING

PART 1, Questions 1–10

1   central
2   600
3   2 year(s)
4   garage
5   garden
6   study
7   noisy
8   595
9&10   IN EITHER ORDER
    B
    E

PART 2 , Questions 11–20

11   classical music/(classical/music) concerts
12   bookshop/bookstore
13   planned
14   1983/(the) 1980s
15   City Council
16   363
17   (the) Garden Hall
18   Three Lives
19   4.50
20   Faces of China

PART 3, Questions 21–30

21   C
22   C
23   A
24   B
25   C
26   A
27   C
28   A
29   B
30   C

PART 4, Questions 31–40

31   B
32   B
33   B
34   A
35   combination/system
36   safety
37   attitude(s)
38   control(s)
39   factory/factories
40   skills

If you score . . .

0–13	14–28	29–40
you are unlikely to get an acceptable score under examination conditions and we recommend that you spend a lot of time improving your English before you take IELTS.	you may get an acceptable score under examination conditions but we recommend that you think about having more practice or lessons before you take IELTS.	you are likely to get an acceptable score under examination conditions but remember that different institutions will find different scores acceptable.

ACADEMIC READING

Reading Passage 1, Questions 1–13

1 D
2 A
3 A
4 power companies
5 safely
6 size
7 B
8 C
9 G
10 D
11 NO
12 YES
13 NOT GIVEN

Reading Passage 2, Questions 14–26

14–18   *IN ANY ORDER*

　B
　C
　F
　H
　J
19 TRUE

20 TRUE
21 FALSE
22 TRUE
23 TRUE
24 NOT GIVEN
25 TRUE
26 NOT GIVEN

Reading Passage 3, Questions 27–40

27 ix
28 ii
29 vii
30 i
31 viii
32 iv
33&34   *IN EITHER ORDER*
　physical chemistry (and)
　thermodynamics
35 adapt
36 immortality
37 NO
38 YES
39 NOT GIVEN
40 YES

If you score . . .

0–11	12–28	29–40
you are unlikely to get an acceptable score under examination conditions and we recommend that you spend a lot of time improving your English before you take IELTS.	you may get an acceptable score under examination conditions but we recommend that you think about having more practice or lessons before you take IELTS.	you are likely to get an acceptable score under examination conditions but remember that different institutions will find different scores acceptable.

TEST 4

LISTENING

PART 1, Questions 1–10

1	waiter(s)
2	day off
3	break
4	(free) meal
5	dark (coloured/colored)
6	jacket
7	28 June
8	Urwin
9	12.00 (pm)/noon/mid-day
10	reference

PART 2, Questions 11–20

11	A
12	B
13	B
14	C
15	D
16	G
17	B
18	F
19	A
20	E

PART 3, Questions 21–30

21&22 IN EITHER ORDER
   B
   E
23&24 IN EITHER ORDER
   A
   C

25	B
26	C
27	priorities
28	timetable
29	(small) tasks
30	(single) paragraph

PART 4, Questions 31–40

31	C
32	B
33	C
34	A
35	B
36	B
37	animal/creature
38	sea/water level(s)
39	hunting
40	creation

If you score . . .

0–11	12–27	28–40
you are unlikely to get an acceptable score under examination conditions and we recommend that you spend a lot of time improving your English before you take IELTS.	you may get an acceptable score under examination conditions but we recommend that you think about having more practice or lessons before you take IELTS.	you are likely to get an acceptable score under examination conditions but remember that different institutions will find different scores acceptable.

ACADEMIC READING

Reading Passage 1, Questions 1–13

1 vii
2 i
3 v
4 ii
5 viii
6 YES
7 NO
8 NOT GIVEN
9 NO
10 B
11 C
12 A
13 C

Reading Passage 2, Questions 14–26

14 B
15 A
16 D
17 D
18 NOT GIVEN
19 YES
20 NO
21 YES
22 D
23 H
24 C
25 E
26 B

Reading Passage 3, Questions 27–40

27 TRUE
28 NOT GIVEN
29 TRUE
30 FALSE
31 A
32 C
33 B
34 D
35 A
36 D
37 heat
38 leaf litter
39 screen
40 alcohol

If you score . . .

0–11	12–28	29–40
you are unlikely to get an acceptable score under examination conditions and we recommend that you spend a lot of time improving your English before you take IELTS.	you may get an acceptable score under examination conditions but we recommend that you think about having more practice or lessons before you take IELTS.	you are likely to get an acceptable score under examination conditions but remember that different institutions will find different scores acceptable.

GENERAL TRAINING TEST A

Section 1, Questions 1–14

1	C
2	B
3	A
4	(for/in) May
5	*IN EITHER ORDER; BOTH REQUIRED FOR ONE MARK*
	canoeing (and)
	tennis
6	(by) (self-drive) auto(mobile)
7	A
8	B
9	D
10	D
11	C
12	B
13	D
14	C

Section 2, Questions 15–27

15	senior
16	(to) search
17	disciplinary action
18	contractors
19	outsiders
20	(private) notes
21	(in) 2003
22	4 weeks (a year)
23	one twelfth (of annual holiday(s))
24	(equal) counter-notice
25	(the) (annual) shutdown/(a) shutdown
26	(a) (holiday) payment/outstanding holiday payment
27	(a) collective agreement

Section 3, Questions 28–40

28	v
29	vii
30	ix
31	x
32	iii
33	iv
34	FALSE
35	NOT GIVEN
36	TRUE
37	FALSE
38	TRUE
39	NOT GIVEN
40	TRUE

If you score . . .

0–15	16–30	31–40
you are unlikely to get an acceptable score under examination conditions and we recommend that you spend a lot of time improving your English before you take IELTS.	you may get an acceptable score under examination conditions but we recommend that you think about having more practice or lessons before you take IELTS.	you are likely to get an acceptable score under examination conditions but remember that different institutions will find different scores acceptable.

GENERAL TRAINING TEST B

Section 1, Questions 1–14

1   TRUE
2   FALSE
3   FALSE
4   FALSE
5   NOT GIVEN
6   TRUE
7   NOT GIVEN
8   TRUE
9   D
10 B
11 B
12 B
13 C
14 C

Section 2, Questions 15–27

15 (an) audit/(waste) audit
16 (duplex) printers
17 (educational) posters
18 (regular) newsletters
19 (writing) notes
20 (ceramic) mugs
21 (to) charities
22 (some) politicians
23 formula
24 (company) employees
25 shareholder reports
26 lies
27 benefited/benefitted

Section 3, Questions 28–40

28 TRUE
29 NOT GIVEN
30 NOT GIVEN
31 FALSE
32 A
33 C
34 C
35 B
36 A
37 D
38 E
39 ***IN EITHER ORDER; BOTH REQUIRED FOR ONE MARK***
    A
    C
40 ***IN EITHER ORDER; BOTH REQUIRED FOR ONE MARK***
    B
    F

If you score . . .

0–15	16–30	31–40
you are unlikely to get an acceptable score under examination conditions and we recommend that you spend a lot of time improving your English before you take IELTS.	you may get an acceptable score under examination conditions but we recommend that you think about having more practice or lessons before you take IELTS.	you are likely to get an acceptable score under examination conditions but remember that different institutions will find different scores acceptable.

Model and sample answers for Writing tasks

TEST 1, WRITING TASK 1

MODEL ANSWER

This model has been prepared by an examiner as an example of a very good answer. However, please note that this is just one example out of many possible approaches.

The pie chart shows that there are four main causes of farmland becoming degraded in the world today. Globally, 65% of degradation is caused by too much animal grazing and tree clearance, constituting 35% and 30% respectively. A further 28% of global degradation is due to over-cultivation of crops. Other causes account for only 7% collectively.

These causes affected different regions differently in the 1990s, with Europe having as much as 9.8% of degradation due to deforestation, while the impact of this on Oceania and North America was minimal, with only 1.7% and 0.2% of land affected respectively. Europe, with the highest overall percentage of land degraded (23%), also suffered from over-cultivation (7.7%) and over-grazing (5.5%). In contrast, Oceania had 13% of degraded farmland and this was mainly due to over-grazing (11.3%). North America had a lower proportion of degraded land at only 5%, and the main causes of this were over-cultivation (3.3%) and, to a lesser extent, over-grazing (1.5%).

Overall, it is clear that Europe suffered more from farmland degradation than the other regions, and the main causes there were deforestation and over-cultivation.

TEST 1, WRITING TASK 2

MODEL ANSWER

This model has been prepared by an examiner as an example of a very good answer. However, please note that this is just one example out of many possible approaches.

A child's education has never been about learning information and basic skills only. It has always included teaching the next generation how to be good members of society. Therefore, this cannot be the responsibility of the parents alone.

In order to be a good member of any society the individual must respect and obey the rules of their community and share their values. Educating children to understand the need to obey rules and respect others always begins in the home and is widely thought to be the responsibility of parents. They will certainly be the first to help children learn what is important in life, how they are expected to behave and what role they will play in their world.

However, learning to understand and share the value system of a whole society cannot be achieved just in the home. Once a child goes to school, they are entering a wider community where teachers and peers will have just as much influence as their parents do at home. At school, children will experience working and living with people from a whole variety of backgrounds from the wider society. This experience should teach them how to co-operate with each other and how to contribute to the life of their community.

But to be a valuable member of any community is not like learning a simple skill. It is something that an individual goes on learning throughout life and it is the responsibility of every member of a society to take responsibility for helping the younger generation to become active and able members of that society.

TEST 2, WRITING TASK 1

MODEL ANSWER

This model has been prepared by an examiner as an example of a very good answer. However, please note that this is just one example out of many possible approaches.

The charts show how much a UK school spent on different running costs in three separate years: 1981, 1991 and 2001.

In all three years, the greatest expenditure was on staff salaries. But while other workers' salaries saw a fall from 28% in 1981 to only 15% of spending in 2001, teachers' pay remained the biggest cost, reaching 50% of total spending in 1991 and ending at 45% in 2001.

Expenditure on resources such as books had increased to 20% by 1991 before decreasing to only 9% by the end of the period. In contrast, the cost of furniture and equipment saw an opposite trend. This cost decreased to only 5% of total expenditure in 1991 but rose dramatically in 2001 when it represented 23% of the school budget. Similarly, the cost of insurance saw a rising trend, growing from only 2% to 8% by 2001.

Overall, teachers' salaries constituted the largest cost to the school, and while spending increased dramatically for equipment and insurance, there were corresponding drops in expenditure on things such as books and on other workers' salaries.

TEST 2, WRITING TASK 2

SAMPLE ANSWER

This is an answer written by a candidate who achieved a **Band 5.5** score. Here is the examiner's comment:

The topic introduction has been copied from the task and is deducted from the word count. This leaves the answer underlength at 236 words, so the candidate loses marks for this.

This answer addresses both questions, but the first is not well covered in terms of how actual relationships have changed. Nevertheless, there is a clear opinion that the effects have been positive and relationships have improved, with some relevant ideas to support this. There is a general progression to the argument, with some effective use of time markers and linkers. There is also some repetition, however. Paragraphing is not always logical, and ideas are not always well linked. A range of vocabulary that is relevant to the topic is used, including some precise and natural expressions. There are quite a lot of mistakes in word form, word choice or spelling, but these do not usually reduce understanding. A variety of sentence types is used, but not always accurately. Errors in grammar and punctuation are distracting at times, but only rarely cause problems for the reader.

Nowadays the way people interact with each other has changed because of technology.

Yes, the technology has changed the people's interaction in very enhanced manner.

Earlier people use to wait and try to find easy way to contact their friends or relatives leaving far. In past there was no quick technology to contact or to establish any communication between one person to another person. The Drawback with past communication systems was that it were very slow and were time taking process such as telegrams, letter etc. People used to afraid to write their personal feedbacks or things to their love ones due to insecure medium of communication. When it comes to professional level, the privacy and accuracy should be maintain but, to that time there were no secure communications.

Now the things have changed around, people from far distance contact their loves one in an easy and quick ways which improves the Interaction level between two person. Quality the level of the Interaction between people to people, has improved because the people are equipped with high-tec technology which enhances the communication. There are many many medium which are available now such as Internet, Calling Cards etc.

The technology has provided the mobility faster which help people to talk or to interact at any time anywhere in the world.

People can contact their friend or relatives any time they want. It has become so easier and feriendly to be in touch with your feriends, relatives even with the unknown people.

TEST 3, WRITING TASK 1

SAMPLE ANSWER

This is an answer written by a candidate who achieved a **Band 6** score. Here is the examiner's comment:

> This answer presents the information in the two diagrams appropriately. The main differences between the two processes are identified in a clear summary, but other important features could be described more fully. The organisation of information is the strongest feature of this script. The description is well organised and there is a smooth progression across the whole answer that is achieved through good use of linkers and referencing phrases. A range of relevant vocabulary is used, although this is not wide and there are some less suitable word choices. There are a few mistakes in spelling, but these do not make the answer difficult to understand. A mix of sentence forms is used and there are some accurate examples of complex structures, but the many short, simple sentences tend to limit the range.

The diagrams show the processes and the equipments used to make cement, and how these are used to produce concrete for building purposes.

The first step in the cement productios is to introduce limestone clay. These materials pass through a crusher that produces a powder. Then this powder goes into a mixer. After this, the product passes to a rotating heater which works with heat. Afterwards, the mixture goes into a ginder where the cement comes out. At the end of the process, the cement is packed in bags.

Referring to the concret production, the process begins with a combination of 15% cement, 10% water, 25% and sand 50% gravel. These four elements are introduced into a concrete mixer.

As mentioned above, the concrete production takes fewer steps that the cement production; however, it is necessary to use more materials than the latter process in order to obtain the final product.

The last difference between both processes is that the concrete mixer does not work with heat.

TEST 3, WRITING TASK 2

MODEL ANSWER

This model has been prepared by an examiner as an example of a very good answer. However, please note that this is just one example out of many possible approaches.

There is no doubt that traffic and pollution from vehicles have become huge problems, both in cities and on motorways everywhere. Solving these problems is likely to need more than a simple rise in the price of petrol.

While it is undeniable that private car use is one of the main causes of the increase in traffic and pollution, higher fuel costs are unlikely to limit the number of drivers for long. As this policy would also affect the cost of public transport, it would be very unpopular with everyone who needs to travel on the roads. But there are various other measures that could be implemented that would have a huge effect on these problems.

I think to tackle the problem of pollution, cleaner fuels need to be developed. The technology is already available to produce electric cars that would be both quieter and cleaner to use. Persuading manufacturers and travellers to adopt this new technology would be a more effective strategy for improving air quality, especially in cities.

However, traffic congestion will not be solved by changing the type of private vehicle people can use. To do this, we need to improve the choice of public transport services available to travellers. For example, if sufficient sky trains and underground train systems were built and effectively maintained in our major cities, then traffic on the roads would be dramatically reduced. Long-distance train and coach services should be made attractive and affordable alternatives to driving your own car for long journeys.

In conclusion, I think that long-term traffic and pollution reductions would depend on educating the public to use public transport more, and on governments using public money to construct and run efficient systems.

TEST 4, WRITING TASK 1

SAMPLE ANSWER

This is an answer written by a candidate who achieved a **Band 8** score. Here is the examiner's comment:

This answer covers all the relevant information in the task, and clearly highlights the main trends and comparisons. The only thing that would improve this answer is an introduction to the topic that is not so closely copied from the prompt.

The message is easy to follow because paragraphing is logical and information is clearly linked across the whole answer. A wide range of vocabulary is used accurately and effectively, although there are some rare imprecise choices and some repetitions. Similarly, a wide range of grammatical structures and sentence forms is used accurately and effectively, with only one significant error where punctuation is omitted in the final paragraph. Overall, most sentences are accurate.

The graph illustrates the quantities of goods transported in the United Kingdom by four different modes of transport between the time period of 1974 and 2002. Over this span of 28 years, the quantities of goods transported by road, water and pipeline have all increased while the quantity transported by rail has remained almost constant at about 40 million tonnes.

The largest quantity of goods transported both in 1974 and 2002 was by road (70 million tonnes and 98 million tonnes respectively) while the lowest both in 1974 and 2002 was by pipeline (about 5 million tonnes and 22 million tonnes respectively). The amount of goods transported by water was constant from 1974 to 1978, where it showed an exponential growth, rising to almost 60 million tonnes after which it plateaued for about 20 years before starting to rise gradually again.

The amount of goods transported by rail is almost constant at 40 million tonnes in 1974 and 2002, with decreases in quantity in between the years. It is also interesting to note that almost all showed a decrease in 1994 in amount of goods transported except for the pipeline, which actually peaked in that year.

In conclusion the road remains the most popular method of transporting goods in the UK while water and pipelines are becoming increasingly used, have not become more popular as a method of transport.

TEST 4, WRITING TASK 2

SAMPLE ANSWER

This is an answer written by a candidate who achieved a **Band 6.5** score. Here is the examiner's comment:

This script answers both parts of the task and presents a clear opinion on the issues. There are relevant main ideas, although the supporting examples are sometimes less appropriate. The answer is organised with some good use of connectives and time-markers giving an overall progression to the argument. There are also mistakes, however, and some lack of linking between sentences. Paragraphing is used, but is not always logical, and the concluding paragraph is confused. The range of vocabulary is the best feature of this script, and includes some good use of natural expressions and idiomatic language. There is some inappropriate use of a less formal style at times, but control is generally good. There are few word choices that are inaccurate, and errors in word form and spelling are only occasional. A variety of sentence forms is used with accuracy and fluency, but there are a lot of short, simple sentences that reduce the range of complex structures. There are grammatical errors and omissions, but these are not frequent.

In some countries the average weight of people is increasing and their levels of health and fitness are decreasing. I think that the cause of these problems are due to unhealthy lifestyle and the lack of exercise.

Nowadays, people are getting more and more lazy. They want convience in everything. When they come home from work, they will have microwaved dinner or fast food so that they do not have to take the trouble to prepare a meal or wash up after dinner. The introduction of fast food is also the main cause of unhealthy living. People are opting a fast food restaurant meal rather than a simple homecooked meal. Yes, your burgers and pizzas tasted better than a homecooked meal but think of all the calories you are swallowing. The oil they used to fry your fries. It is literally black. Eating too much fast food will also lead to health problems. Sugary drinks, packeted chips, candies and chocolate are also some of the causes that contributes to unhealthy lifestyle. Heavy consumption can lead to weight gain and diabeties.

I think that the main cause is the lack of exercise. As you grow older, your metabolism rate drops. Even if you are eating the same amount as before, you will still gain weight. The one and only solution to this is exercise. The recommended exercise per day is at least 30 minutes of brisk walking. This target can be easily achieved if people do not drive to work. They can take a bus or a train and drip one stop earlier than walk to the office. Every little bit counts. When you comes home from work, you can play with your kids or bring the dog for a walk. Anything to get your attention away from the couch. More exercise will surpress your cravings for sugary stuffs.

People should also balance their diet. For example, by eating more vegetables and fruits. Eat less meat and drink plenty of water throughout the day. Organise time with your family to take a walk outdoors to enjoy the sceneries rather than cooping yourself in the house. This is healthy living for the body, heart and the soul. It is also less likely to fall sick if you do plenty of exercise as your body is strong enough to fight off illness and diseases.

TEST A, WRITING TASK 1 (GENERAL TRAINING)

MODEL ANSWER

This model has been prepared by an examiner as an example of a very good answer. However, please note that this is just one example out of many possible approaches.

> Dear Dave,
>
> I am writing to let you know that at last we have moved to a bigger house! We just couldn't go on living in the two-bedroom bungalow now that the twins are growing up and the new baby has arrived. So we started looking – and one thing led to another and finally here we are in our new home.
>
> I'm sure you'll like it. We have three bedrooms now, and a very modern bathroom and kitchen. The kids are happy because there is much more space with the big living room and the garden outside. But Michel is the happiest of all because he doesn't need to do much decorating.
>
> Why don't you come round this weekend and see what you think of our new place? We would all love to see you and if the weather is good we can have a barbecue in the garden.
>
> Our new address and phone number are below, so give us a call and let us know when to expect you.
>
> Lots of love,
>
> Françoise

TEST A, WRITING TASK 2 (GENERAL TRAINING)

SAMPLE ANSWER

This is an answer written by a candidate who achieved a **Band 7** score. Here is the examiner's comment:

This script is from a very high-level candidate who does not read the task carefully and who loses marks for this and for a lack of paragraphing.

This answer is a sophisticated response to the first question in the task. Reasons for increases in both long-distance and local travel are analysed and argued. However, the second question on the benefits for the traveller is not addressed at all, so the task is only partially answered and this limits the rating. Although the answer is logically organised and ideas are well linked, unfortunately there is no attempt at paragraphing. This makes it more difficult for the reader to identify the main points in the argument. A wide range of language is used naturally and accurately. There are no noticeable mistakes in the use of vocabulary or grammar and only rare lapses in the use of punctuation and spelling. Otherwise, the writer has full control of the language used.

Today more people are travelling than ever before. The reasons for this increase are many and varied. On a simplistic level, there are larger numbers of means of transportation – there are more cars, buses and trains in operation. However, the sheer number of transportation means is not enough to explain this increase. The cost of travelling; even though it is at present increasing due to an economic slow-down globally; is still relatively affordable to many people. This affordability is further enhanced by the use of credit cards and loans in order to fund travel, especially for holiday purposes. An increase of travel companies in competition with each other has also helped bring package prices down, while an increase in the number of operating flights globally has also increased, giving rise to falling air-fare prices. In addition, people now have more leisure time and disposable incomes. The combination of these two variables with unrelenting advertising campaigns from travel companies and cruise ship operators arguably leads to an increase in the number of people travelling, in this case for holiday purposes. Another reason why people travel is going to work. More than ever before, people are travelling greater distances to get to work. Large industrial sites for both service and production industries are tending to be located outside city areas. This invariably leads to increases in the number of people travelling locally. In conclusion, there are many reasons why more people are travelling both internationally and locally, for business and for leisure. What is sure is that this increase is likely to continue until travelling at current rates is no longer economically viable.

TEST B, WRITING TASK 1 (GENERAL TRAINING)

SAMPLE ANSWER

This is an answer written by a candidate who achieved a **Band 4.5** score. Here is the examiner's comment:

> The answer addresses the task and, although the response to bullet two is limited and not wholly focused on the prompt, the letter has a clear purpose. The points are organised but do not flow well because the progression is not always signalled clearly. Ideas can be linked, but there is only limited use of connectives, and these are not always accurate. Vocabulary is also limited, with mistakes in even basic words so the reader has to make some effort to follow the meaning. Similarly, control of sentence structure and grammar is weak, and punctuation is not used accurately. There are some correct structures, but errors are very frequent and are confusing for the reader.

Dear Sir or Madam,

I am writing this Letter to explain my problem which recently I bought dish From your shops, then it is broke.

Last week I bought a small piece of dish For my kitchen and I got warranty for that, when I current it to my home suddenly when I walking on the street I heared something is broke, then, I opened my bag, unfortunately my dish is broke and I think It was changed because that piece Like old and not that piece which I saw in first time. I call your shop several times, but, unfortunately no answer from your shop.

I would be greatful If you returen my money or changed this piece, Allso, I like to talk with that man who changed my dish and I would Like from you to stoped hem for short time for his Job.

faithfully

TEST B, WRITING TASK 2 (GENERAL TRAINING)

MODEL ANSWER

This model has been prepared by an examiner as an example of a very good answer. However, please note that this is just one example out of many possible approaches.

Some countries have single-sex education models, while in others both single sex and mixed schools co-exist and it is up to the parents or the children to decide which model is preferable.

Some educationalists think it is more effective to educate boys and girls in single-sex schools because they believe this environment reduces distractions and encourages pupils to concentrate on their studies. This is probably true to some extent. It also allows more equality among pupils and gives more opportunity to all those at the school to choose subjects more freely without gender prejudice. For example, a much higher proportion of girls study science to a high level when they attend girls' schools than their counterparts in mixed schools do. Similarly, boys in single-sex schools are more likely to take cookery classes and to study languages, which are often thought of as traditional subjects for girls.

On the other hand, some experts would argue that mixed schools prepare their pupils better for their future lives. Girls and boys learn to live and work together from an early age and are consequently not emotionally underdeveloped in their relations with the opposite sex. They are also able to learn from each other, and to experience different types of skill and talent than might be evident in a single gender environment.

Personally, I think that there are advantages to both systems. I went to a mixed school, but feel that I myself missed the opportunity to specialise in science because it was seen as the natural domain and career path for boys when I was a girl. So because of that, I would have preferred to go to a girls' school. But hopefully times have changed, and both genders of student can have equal chances to study what they want to in whichever type of school they attend.

Sample answer sheets

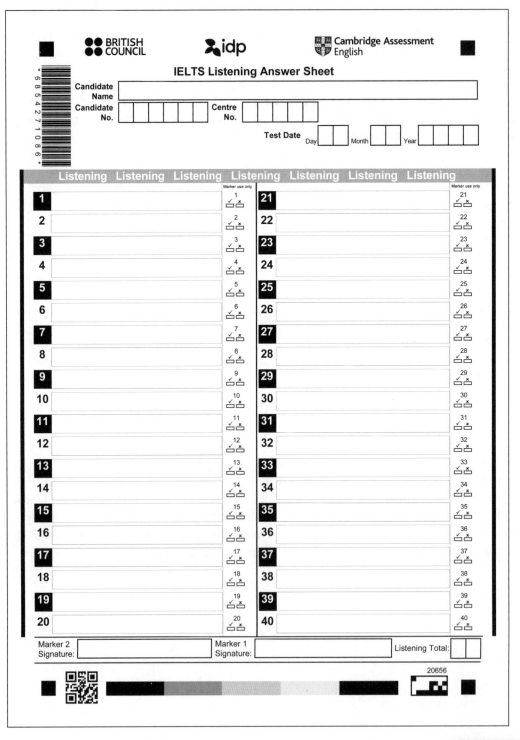

BRITISH COUNCIL **idp** **Cambridge Assessment English**

IELTS Reading Answer Sheet

Candidate Name

Candidate No.

Centre No.

Test Module ☐ Academic ☐ General Training

Test Date Day Month Year

Reading Reading Reading Reading Reading Reading Reading

	Marker use only			Marker use only
1	1 ✓ ✗	**21**		21 ✓ ✗
2	2 ✓ ✗	**22**		22 ✓ ✗
3	3 ✓ ✗	**23**		23 ✓ ✗
4	4 ✓ ✗	**24**		24 ✓ ✗
5	5 ✓ ✗	**25**		25 ✓ ✗
6	6 ✓ ✗	**26**		26 ✓ ✗
7	7 ✓ ✗	**27**		27 ✓ ✗
8	8 ✓ ✗	**28**		28 ✓ ✗
9	9 ✓ ✗	**29**		29 ✓ ✗
10	10 ✓ ✗	**30**		30 ✓ ✗
11	11 ✓ ✗	**31**		31 ✓ ✗
12	12 ✓ ✗	**32**		32 ✓ ✗
13	13 ✓ ✗	**33**		33 ✓ ✗
14	14 ✓ ✗	**34**		34 ✓ ✗
15	15 ✓ ✗	**35**		35 ✓ ✗
16	16 ✓ ✗	**36**		36 ✓ ✗
17	17 ✓ ✗	**37**		37 ✓ ✗
18	18 ✓ ✗	**38**		38 ✓ ✗
19	19 ✓ ✗	**39**		39 ✓ ✗
20	20 ✓ ✗	**40**		40 ✓ ✗

Marker 2 Signature:

Marker 1 Signature:

Reading Total:

61788

Acknowledgements

The authors and publishers acknowledge the following sources of copyright material and are grateful for the permissions granted. While every effort has been made, it has not always been possible to identify the sources of all the material used, or to trace all copyright holders. If any omissions are brought to our notice, we will be happy to include the appropriate acknowledgements on reprinting.

Cengage Learning for the adapted text on pp. 23−24 'Air Traffic Control in the USA' from *World of Invention*. Copyright © 1999 Gale, a part of Cengage Learning, Inc. Reproduced by permission. www.cengage.com/permissions; Perseus Books Group for the adapted text on pp. 46−47 'The Little Ice Age' from *The Little Ice Age* by Brian Fagan, published by Perseus Books Group, 2001; Taylor & Francis Books, UK for the adapted text on pp. 50−51 'The meaning and power of smell' from *Aroma: A Cultural History of Smell* by Constance Classen, published by Routledge 1994. Reproduced by permission of Taylor & Francis Books, UK; New Scientist Magazine for the adapted text on pp. 65−66 'Striking Back at Lightning with Lasers' from 'Striking Back at Lightning' by Hazel Muir, *New Scientist Magazine* 7 October 1995. Copyright © New Scientist Magazine; Colin Tyre for the adapted text on pp.70−71 'The Nature of Genius' from *Gifted or Able? Realising Children's Potential* by Colin Tyre and Peter Young (decd), published by Open University Press, 1992. Reproduced with permission; Taylor & Francis Group for the adapted text on pp. 89−90 'Land of the Rising Sum' from 'The Teaching of Mathematics in Japan: an English perspective', from *Oxford Review of Education* Vol 21, no 3 1995, pp. 347−360 by Julia Whitburn. Reproduced by permission of Taylor & Francis Group; 'Biological Control of Pests' on pp. 93−94 from 'Biological control of pests gaining popularity' by Radhakrishna Rao *The Straits Times* 1989; CSIRO Ecosystems Sciences for the adapted text on pp. 97−98 'Collecting Ant Specimens' from the website: http://www.csiro. au/. Reproduced with permission; 'Recycling at work – handy hints to employers' on pp. 121−122 from 'Handy hints for recycling at work', The States of Jersey website; Shiree Schumacher for the adapted text on pp. 125−126 'Talking Point' from 'Talking Point' *NEXT Magazine (NZ)*, July 2001. Reproduced with permission.

Photo Acknowledgements

p. 18: Science Museum; p. 87: iStock/© Patrick Ellis; p. 97: Shutterstock/orionmystery@flickr; p. 113: Shutterstock/Frank Jr; p. 121: iStock/© Adam Brown; p. 123: Shutterstock/Alexander Raths.

Design concept by Peter Ducker MSTD.

Cover design by David Lawton.

The audio CDs which accompany this book were recorded at dsound, London.

Page make up by Servis Filmsetting Ltd, Stockport, Cheshire.